Y0-BRO-490

Cultural Otherness

Correspondence with Richard Rorty

The American Academy of Religion
Cultural Criticism Series

Number 4

CULTURAL OTHERNESS:
CORRESPONDENCE WITH RICHARD RORTY

Second Edition

Anindita Niyogi Balslev

Cultural Otherness

Correspondence with Richard Rorty

Second Edition

Anindita Niyogi Balslev

Scholars Press
Atlanta

CULTURAL OTHERNESS:
CORRESPONDENCE WITH RICHARD RORTY

Copyright © 1991 by the
Indian Institute of Advanced Study

Preface to second edition copyright © 1999 by the
American Academy of Religion

All Rights Reserved.

No part of this work may be reproduced or transmitted in any form or by any means, electronic or mechanical, including photocopying and recording, or by means of any information storage or retrieval system, except as may be expressly permitted by the 1976 Copyright Act or in writing from the publisher. Requests for permission should be addressed in writing to the Rights and Permissions Department, Scholars Press, P.O. Box 15399, Atlanta, GA 30333-0399, USA.

Library of Congress Cataloging-in-Publication Data

Balslev, Anindita Niyogi.
    Cultural otherness, correspondence with Richard Rorty / Anindita Niyogi Balslev. – 2nd ed.
        p.   cm. – (The American Academy of Religion cultural criticism series ; no. 4)
    Includes bibliographical references.
    ISBN 0-7885-0300-6 (paper : acid-free paper)
    1. Cross-cultural orientation–Philosophy.   2. Rorty, Richard–Correspondence.   I. Title.   II. Series.
GN345.65.B35   1999
306'.01–dc21   99-38046
                                                                                                                 CIP

Richard Rorty's essay "Philosophers, Novelists, and Intercultural Comparisons: Heidegger, Kundera, and Dickens" was first published in *Essays in Heidegger and Others*, Volume 2 of his *Philosophical Papers* (Cambridge and New York: Cambridge University Press, 1991), and is reprinted here with the permission of Cambridge University Press.

This book is printed on recycled, acid-free paper.

99 00 01 02 03 04 05 06 07 08 — 10 9 8 7 6 5 4 3 2 1

MANUFACTURED IN THE UNITED STATES OF AMERICA

For Eva and Olav, Patricia and Kevin

Contents

Preface

When one stands, as I do, at the crossroads of cultures, one becomes aware that questions about cultural issues cannot be dealt with adequately in a monologue or even in a dialogue with an imaginary or projected other. Rather, they require an open conversation. As a scholar, I have felt the lack of this active interchange of ideas in the areas of philosophy as well as in religious and cultural studies. Several years ago I initiated an exchange of letters with Professor Richard Rorty, precisely with the hope of creating an intellectual space (and eventually of setting up a forum) where it will be possible to truly engage in a conversation about a range of issues that present themselves when one stands at the intersection of cultures. This correspondence took place in the interval between two conferences sponsored by Philosophy East-West, one held in Hawaii in 1989 and the other in India in 1991. The resulting letters were first published in India by the Indian Institute of Advanced Study in 1991. Since then many readers, both outside and inside the academia, have encouraged their republication in the U.S. They appear here in the American Academy of Religion's Cultural Criticism Series by the kind permission of the Indian Institute and Professor Rorty himself. This volume also contains the essay by Rorty to which many of my own and Rorty's remarks refer.

At the outset, a few remarks about the title of this book may be in order. The theme of "cultural otherness" has a definitive contemporary relevance. An increasing sharing of advanced technology has significantly reduced distances between the remotest parts of the globe during the twentieth century, allowing the catch phrase "global village" to appear in all sorts of discourses. As a consequence of this, however, our awareness of the conceptual and cultural distances that still divide us has augmented considerably. We often speak, especially in academia, about the difficulties of crossing cultural boundaries and about the "otherness" of the other. This new closeness has also made us conscious of the persistence of commitments to religious beliefs and traditions in many segments of society and different parts of the world, thus putting into relief the major importance of a genuine encounter of world religions.

It is true of course that a great variety of difficulties arise from our new proximity, difficulties of concern to both dominant and marginal groups. These occur not only in the context of huge complexes of culture designated as East and West or North and South (or any other actual and possible modes of conceiving blocks in terms of cultural differences or political economy alone), but also within any given culture, more aware of the boundaries of gender, religion, ethnicity, race, and political ideology than ever before. However, while engaging in discussion of any aspect of the problems posed by the plurality of cultures and subcultures, we need to question the hard sense of the metaphor of boundary that divides one from the other. When the metaphor of boundary implies impermeable barrier, it is not conducive to the kind of conversation I have in mind, as this actually creates a space where old ignorance continues and new cliches prevail. The soft sense of the metaphor, on the other hand, is indeed useful. This allows us to acknowledge differences without jeopardizing communication.[1]

As a pertinent example, and one with important implications also for religious studies, let me focus on the manner in which the so-called otherness of the Indian philosophical traditions has been and still is projected by significant philosophers in the West. Since I have briefly mentioned this point in one of my letters to Professor Rorty, let me elaborate on this a bit more here as I believe that the lack of conversation between India and the West is most glaring among philosophers. Although many on the Indian subcontinent are unaware of the fact that there is any problem with representing *darśana* (or *ānvīkṣikī*) as *philosophy*, mainstream Western self-understanding has always posited that philosophy is a unique creation of the Greeks and consequently that it is an exclusive enterprise of those who are the direct inheritors of that culture. Notable Western philosophers such as Hegel, Husserl, and Heidegger—to take only the most prominent examples—have all denied that there is in the East any project of thinking at all like that of Greek *philosophia*.

Occasionally those who knew better have protested against this view,[2] and historical forces have gradually brought us to the phase when, despite doubts and scorns about the search for philosophy elsewhere than in the West, accounts of the intellectual adventure in the Indian subcontinent have become available as histories of Indian philosophy, written in European languages by both Western and Indian scholars.[3] In the course of time scholars from both sides of this apparent divide between these traditions have carried on the daring adventure of relating and contrasting specific philosophical themes, suspending their sense of the hard boundaries of various traditions of thought. Consequently the project of "comparative philosophy" has become increasingly visible. Despite difficulties, this enterprise is now open to crosscultural philosophical reflections, in the course of which scholars struggle to establish their claims through historical scholarship and analysis, rather than by *a priori* argumentation and cultural clichés that shun genuine confrontation with actual historical unfolding of thought-traditions.

Nevertheless, the conservative attitudes seem to remain a dominant mode of self-understanding of those who continue with the mainstream Western philosophical tradition. These attitudes account in part for the persistent indifference toward Eastern thought in the academic offerings of the philosophy departments in the West. To be reluctant to examine this question is to continue uncritically with old prejudices that perpetuate the image of the "mythical, mysterious, non-rational East."[4] Thinking about our "global village," one is tempted to hope that the days are finally over when it was commonplace to describe the huge complexes of cultures in diagrammatically opposed terms, such as those old stereotypes of the East as "spiritual" and the West as "materialistic." Yet one still hears the voice of philosophers describing the West as a "culture of hope" and the East as a "culture of endurance."[5] As an observer of such clichés, I find a conspicuous lack of balance in the way we perceive each other, a lack of comprehension that generates a number of our failures to establish the conditions for fruitful social and intellectual negotiations in a global context.

Given the scenario of contemporary technological civilization and the sense of differences and boundaries it creates, both for good and for ill, it is important to take up the question of how to generate a creative and a critical crosscultural discourse, not only by challenging stereotypes about cultures and sub-cultures in general and traditions of thought in particular but by being careful not to entirely abolish the common ground on which they can be addressed. Above all, we must shun the monologue—or even the halfway house of the implied dialogue with a projected other—in favor of genuine, living exchange.

My sense of the need for an open conversation along these lines is born of my awareness of the intellectual vacuum which is created when concerns for mutual understanding are addressed without actually hearing or including the voice of the other in the same forum. In my view, we must not only consistently seek out this other voice, but actively avoid strategies and occasions of the interpretation of "otherness" where the absence or silence of the other is assumed to make no difference. The conviction that is at work here, at least on my part, is that if we are to seek a higher level of critical self-understanding and to engage ourselves in redescribing human relationships, it is not enough that we simply speak *about* others or even *to* others—we have to get ready to speak *with* each other.

Thinking of academia in particular, if universities are not to be ivory towers and educators not to be simply arm-chair intellectuals, there must be made room for an on-going conversation which reflects the issues and concerns of our time that have clear cross-cultural dimensions. Our institutions must provide opportunities in this respect for the next generation to grow up somewhat differently from the way their elders have done. If existing structures of knowledge and power just remain static and the potency of the educational channel is not fully explored in new directions, nothing will be achieved. We will be stuck with wishing for a "new world-order" to emerge without a clear sense of what that order might be. While I am here primarily interested in the theoretical issues having bearing on philosophical and religious studies, I take seriously the point that pragmatist philosophers such as Rorty make when they say that philosophical problems "are disguised forms of practical problems." I also seek to observe the maxim that states that if a set of ideas do "not make any difference to our practices, they make no difference at all."

It is indeed urgent to recognize the crucial importance of crosscultural conversation in the domain of religious studies, which deals with a discourse with great potential for misunderstanding and violence at both the theoretical and practical levels. Some scholars, however, are of the opinion that it is not quite so easy to achieve a Gadamarian fusion of horizons in crosscultural contexts, especially involving religion, where force, power, and violence are always creating different sorts of asymmetries.[6] I agree that certain social and political conditions facilitate the task of engaging in hermeneutical understanding of different cultures. However, my belief is that instead of taking these desired sociopolitical conditions as prerequisites for a possible and a proper intercultural exchange and simply waiting for such a situation to come about, those who from both the hemispheres are acutely sensing this intellectual vacuum must begin to break the silence *even before these ideal conditions obtain.*

Certainly, the asymmetries of which we are aware today will not disappear of their own accord, even in a relatively peaceful context. In order to comprehend the deficiencies in theory-making as well as in practical policy-making, the parties involved need to converse candidly. Furthermore, to speak for a moment theoretically, it does not seem to me possible to conceive *a priori* of a transcultural interpretive strategy for analyzing the immanent structure of cultures, let alone while highlighting religious themes. What is needed is a multi-layered narrative, as it were, in order to confront the subtleties and complexities of the cross-cultural encounter. As we gradually become proficient enough in this conversation to focus on lived encounters and situations, we will be able to unpack the cultural baggage that interpreters carry while weaving theories about philosophy, religion and a wide variety of other topics. One process cannot proceed without the other.

For these and many other reasons, educational institutions are vital places for innovating ways of correcting the basic asymmetries and initiating the crosscultural conversations. If forums can be set up where students and teachers of various backgrounds can engage in conversation precisely with the intention of raising those issues about which they usually remain silent (only to pave the way for later violent eruptions), they might well be seen as effective social investment. This emphasis may also help us better to construe the relation of various institutions (be that for social, political or religious purposes) to society at large. Educational institutions, no matter where these happen to be, are created by the societies they serve, but they also in turn empower these societies and help to change as well as to maintain the status quo. These are mutually reenforcing processes. In the case of educational policy-making, for example, if the educational policy makers could exert some influence in highlighting those concerns which now lie at the periphery of educational programs in philosophy, religion, etc., and help bring them more and more to the center, they would make a difference to the society as a whole.

Let me return to the issue of persistent stereotyping. Even in locations which we presume to be edifying and progressive, such as academia, many clichés prevail. As an example, let me probe more deeply into the contemporary practice of teaching and doing philosophy at the university level and into the inept manner in which the concerns of diverse intellectual traditions are actually represented there. This will help to show why the deliberate and conscious fostering of crosscultural conversation in the sense I am calling for is necessary. I use the word "philosophers" here to refer to those who carry on the task of doing philosophy as a vocation in the formal academic departments of philosophy, usually in a university context. I might remark in passing that only a small number of professional philosophers—and this, I am afraid, holds true conspicuously of the West—have taken the pains to look elsewhere for conceptual resources outside of their cultural horizon, resources which could be fruitful not only for their understanding and appreciation of alternative modes of thinking but for the enrichment of their own pursuits, however classically conceived. Certainly, the standard curriculum pertaining to the discipline of philosophy in the West displays (with very few exceptions) a dearth of representation of other intellectual traditions, which though relevant are considered alien. The perpetuation of this practice maintains precisely the prejudices we must go beyond.

In this connection, let me also observe that we need to comprehend that the geographical demarcation of philosophical thinking that has produced such nomenclatures as "American Pragmatism," "German Idealism," "French Existentialism," or "Indian Vedanta" should not be taken to indicate that only a native can have access to these or produce good work within these schools of thought. There are several examples of scholars who have been recognized as significant interpreters of a given tradition to which they had nothing of that *prima facie* claim to authority which is generally granted almost as a birthright to those who are considered insiders. Indeed, initiation into intellectual traditions outside of one's own cultural horizon might lead to fresh challenges helpful for creative thinking.

Furthermore, a total lack of familiarity with major intellectual traditions of other cultures is particularly conducive to misleading conceptual constructions based upon clichés about the "otherness" of such traditions. A scholar who is deeply committed to more than one tradition of thinking, who knows enough about the gropings, the conflicts, the divergent directions and the multiple levels of thinking that are at work in each of these, learns to exercise caution about received ideas. To give an example from my own research, while attempting to situate the various Indian views about time in an intercultural context, I had to grapple repeatedly with the misconceptions stemming from the persistent cliché that the Indian conception of time is cyclic as opposed to that of Judaism and Christianity, which is described as linear.[7] In wrestling with this issue, I was able to see at first hand how a misuse of these metaphorical designations for describing the various cultural experiences of time can be a serious obstacle for encounters between world religions. In this case, the problem was intensified by the way in which these metaphors had gotten associated with the ideas of progress and salvation. Thus, it was commonplace to stress the "otherness" of adherents of the so-

15

called cyclic time by denying them a sense of history, progress and so forth. Removing this obstacle to serious crosscultural comparison is only one instance of the work of dismantling old stereotypes that enable us to reengage with one another along new lines. Crosscultural projects badly need such endeavors as these stereotypes act as barriers that obstruct philosophical understanding and interreligious communication.[8]

Such work is also vital to a deeper academic involvement with the question of religious pluralism. Evidently, the nuclear age has not turned out to be so postreligious an era as some might have predicted. World religions are still the major sources of ideas which provide meaning and a sense of direction to millions. They play a significant role in the constitution of collective identity over and against the "otherness" of others, a process which is so charged that world religions can indeed be considered powerful determinants of collective behavior. As we know, these religions not only unify, they also divide. A creative and vigorous conversation on religious pluralism needs to draw on the awareness that whichever strategies have been tried so far to underplay or eliminate this plurality have not worked. However, to affirm pluralism while denying the possibility of interreligious communication on the basis that each religion is impermeably "other" to the others also leads to a blind alley. As with philosophy, a deeper acquaintance with traditions other than one's own may be an effective tool for avoiding some of the clichés and stereotypes that everywhere cause immense social distress. The challenge is how to expose to our reflective gaze the distinct core of religious meaning incorporated in the various traditions without rendering them so opaque to one another that no conversation is possible.

The pursuit of crosscultural philosophical and religious ideas is, however, complex and it is especially so when these have clear social and political parameters and imports. One of the anxieties that beset a scholar engaged in this endeavor is whether the kinds of interpretive activities that such a task involves does cultural violence to its methods and objects of study. I am thinking of the concern that Rorty raises when he asks whether in pursuing this endeavor we are really "exchanging ideas or merely courtesies, whether we are genuinely bickering or just staging the kind of ritual characteristic of what Lévi-Strauss has called "UNESCO cosmopolitanism."[9] Rorty expresses the anxiety here that the task of intercultural comparison might be seen as trivial or even point-less, since there is no way for us to know another's point of view with the kind of precision and range of reference that an internal argument about philosophy and religion can have. The problem with this concern, which seems so legitimate on first look, is that it may easily lead to contentions and arguments which amount to an ethnocentric view of philosophy itself. In this connection, it is worthwhile to examine a few of Rorty's own best formulated forebodings along these lines in order to demonstrate how these misgivings actually reenforce an ethnocentric slant to the philo-sophical enterprise as such instead of elucidating the potential for intellectual adventure that a study of philosophy across the boundaries of cultures can be.

In his review of Gerald J. Larson and Eliot Deutsch (eds.), *Interpreting Across Boundaries: New Essays in Comparative Philosophy* (Princeton: Princeton University Press, 1988), Rorty argues that there is no "uncontroversial starting point for comparing forms of intellectual life." Hence any attempt to construct such a "skyhook which will take us out of this parochialism" is in his view vain. Thus, we can never be sure while interpreting philosophies, such as "when we start imposing the grid of our own needs upon non-Westerners." There is no way for us, he maintains, "to come up with right or wrong answers . . . [for] we only have right or wrong answers when we are all agreed about the 'point' of the inquiry." Rorty denies in general, of course, the possibility that "we should ever agree on the 'point' of philosophy." It seems to me, however, that the same sort of observations can be made about any particular rendition of philosophical thinking *within* the frame-work of any given tradition and that it does not have any special bearing on crosscultural projects. Thus, such questions as to whether we are imposing the grid of our own needs in order to interpret a philosopher or as to whether there is any agreed point of inquiry in philosophy or not are not the special burdens of the philosophers involved in crosscultural projects but instead com-mon problems for us all. There is of course serious disagreement among philosophers about these problems, and about Rorty's own way of comprehending philosophy as a project of thinking. Furthermore, I would like to insist in this regard that we need not confine ourselves to the idea that studying philosophies or religions as a crosscultural project has the one and only function of finding similarities and differences in the diverse set of materials that are available to us. If we get stuck with this sense of the enterprise, the charge that this kind of intellectual struggle is nothing more than "a feat of imaginative recontextualization" as Rorty puts it, can hardly be dispelled.

There are indeed other ways of pursuing crosscultural conversation. Personally, I have drawn much intellectual nourishment from working simultaneously in Western and Indian philosophical traditions. While specializing in the area of Indian philosophy, it has often seemed to me that an approach, analysis or method from a tradition of thought that does not owe its origin to the Indian soil was highly useful for a reinterpretation of Indian thought. If a genuine involvement with the sources of Indian thought, its concern, its analytical tools is essential for understanding and creative advancement of the indigenous tradition, it is neither necessary nor advisable to close off the possibilities of interpretation beyond that tradition's already achieved self-understanding.

In other words, as I construe it, learning about another tradition of thought is not the same as constructing an effigy of the otherness of the "other" through imaginative manipulation or merely of identifying spotty and isolated cases of similarity and difference but a matter of letting the "other" speak and then attempting to comprehend what is said. This basic process must proceed whenever a scholar encounters two or more sets of ideas. A continued effort to focus on the shared as well as diverse concerns of various intellectual traditions will enrich the participants who undertake this adventure. Moreover, this exploration alone can foster a sense of a community among philosophers in the global context. A philosophical intervention in the depiction of "cultural otherness" with regard to a wide range of themes is, undoubtedly, one important way that philosophers can help build bridges between cultures that are lacking at present.

One reason for bringing up this discussion is to draw attention to how a limited philosophical self-understanding can account for the relative failure of decades of efforts to enlarge the content of the curriculum in the departments of philosophy in the West. Let me elaborate on this a bit in order to clarify in what way the self-understanding of the philosophical project that Rorty is depicting bears upon this practical situation. The scenario is as follows: Philosophers in the modern West are more often than not university professors. Rorty grants Ninian Smart's claim that "Modern Western philosophy has been a product of a number of cultural accidents, one of which is the institutionalization of universities into a departmental structure." But can the conspicuous absence of the intellectual traditions of the East in these departments be taken as merely another cultural accident? Is it not linked closely to the question still in the air: "Is there philosophy in Asia?"[10] Rorty remarks that this question is "perfectly reasonable to ask, without condescension and in honest bewilderment. . . . For this is not the question 'Is Asia intellectually mature?' but the question 'Have Asians had any of the needs which have lead Western universities to teach Seneca, Ockham, Hume, and Husserl in the same department?'" Yet Rorty does not find it necessary to answer why Heidegger and Quine are taught in the same department when as he himself says in the same review that they "in their professional capacities, felt none of the same needs, pursued almost none of the same purposes."

Granted that one needs to be cautious about the cultural differences which divide philosophical traditions, nevertheless it is regrettable that, given the present-day organization of the educational program in academic departments of philosophy, philosophers like Sankara, Nagarjuna, Diganaga, and Uddyotakara—to mention a few great names at random from the Indian traditions—are not taught in the same departments where such Western figures as Hume, Hegel, or Husserl are venerated. This could help correct some of the asymmetries in crosscultural philosophical exchanges and create a new intellectual space where philosophers could get a more concrete grasp of where the themes and concerns of various traditions of thought overlap and where they do not. This could also give the students of philosophy an opportunity to find out exactly how different the Indian *darśana* tradition is as a thinking project from Greek *philosophia*. This consideration could lead to a further deepening of the question whether we need a plural understanding of what the philosophical enterprise is all about. In any case, it could make it evident that no amount of *a priori* argument can decide such questions as where there is philosophy and where it is nonexistent.

Furthermore, even if we take seriously some of Rorty's forebodings about intercultural comparison in the context of philosophy, I do not see such a project as dispensable. How without it could we identify traditional mistakes that hinder intercultural exchanges? Who can do that job but those who know more than one tradition? It is indeed difficult to ignore the fact that imagined differences often provide the stuff of which cliches about the "otherness" of the others are born.

Thus, in the context of philosophy, and cultural and religious studies alike (concepts which themselves may be open to pluralistic interpretation), one needs to reject the hard sense of the metaphor of boundary that divides intellectual traditions. One needs to avoid thinking of cultural crossing as trespassing, while retaining a sensitivity to the lines that do indeed separate traditions of thought, speech-communities, and social groupings. In any case, to sum up, it is my view that a scholar engaged in such an intellectual adventure cannot accept a theory of culture that lends support to a pernicious form of cultural relativism which claims that divergent intellectual histories lead to closed conceptual worlds among which no communication is possible. This is also why any attempt by scholars to acquaint themselves with such projects of thinking—in no matter what cultural soil—is to be commended as a step toward a veritable intercultural understanding. It expresses, at least, a genuine philosophical need which refuses to limit itself within a single culture, thereby decrying an ethnocentric view of philosophy.

When I pressed this point in my correspondence with Rorty, he made the following interesting remark: "My hunch is that our sense of where to connect up Indian and Western texts will change dramatically when and if people who have read quite a few of both begin to write books which are not clearly identifiable as either Western or Eastern," and this he thinks will "help create a culture within which intellectuals from both sides may meet and communicate." While I appreciate this observation, I take the project of studying the major philosophical traditions of East and West as an integral part of crosscultural conversation and think that this needs to be a part of a legitimate program in an academic setting. Not only does it help identify and expose clichés in the world at large but it may also help to correct some of the oddities that arise from an imbalance of knowledge and power within philosophical, religious and cultural studies themselves. It can perhaps also open up new frontiers and allow us to reconsider the interpretive strategies on cultures that is reflected in the inadequate manner in which traditions of thought have been represented so far, thereby removing the East-West asymmetries in academic exchanges.

It is even possible to imagine that the novel perceptions of an international community of philosophers who know more of each others' traditions would lead not merely to a harvest of bits and pieces of ideas from different thought-traditions but make a new contribution to a genuinely creative philosophy. Who can say that such endeavors will not, in the long run, falsify the prophecy of the "end of philosophy"?

Conscious planning and commitment is, however, badly needed to foster the kind of crosscultural conversation which will lead toward these ends. Crosscultural projects of the kind that I have in mind require the participation not only of professional comparativists, but also of those who, like Rorty, customarily work within the bounded space of their own traditional disciplinary concerns. Only when crosscultural conversation will progress, will it be meaningful to ask how other cultural, religious or philosophical traditions can help to regenerate our own and what techniques and methods are appropriate to understand these other traditions and their potential.

Finally, while dealing with the story of philosophy or religion, one must at the outset keep in mind that the state of any academic discipline—in whatever cultural soil—is by no means free from the influence of factors that condition its over-all cultural history. Read in this vein, it is perhaps now time to let intellectual forces uncover the overlapping contents without underplaying the deviations, the divergences. In this process we will help foster a partnership that does not get thwarted by the talk of radical difference or by the thought of the dissolution of distinctness of a given cultural tradition. Perception of significant but not incommensurable otherness of other traditions of thought, as long as it is based on knowledge and study rather than on a priori assumption, is a philosophically enriching experience to all concerned, whereas repetition of clichés, even when cloaked as recognition of difference, does no one any good.

Notes

1. See Anindita Niyogi Balslev (ed.), *Cross-Cultural Conversation (Initiation)* (Atlanta: Scholars Press, 1996), p. 10.

2. H. von Glasenapp, in his *Indienbild Deutscher Denker* (Stuttgart: K. F. Koehler, 1960), pp. 39ff., described Hegel's reading on India as a caricature and even said that Hegel "ventured on a task for which he was not qualified" (p. 59). Also note the observation of Wilhelm Halbfass in *India And Europe: An Essay in Understanding* (Albany, NY: SUNY Press, 1988), p. 286: "Today, it is no longer necessary to argue that there was philosophy in India in a sense which is fully compatible with what European philosophers were actually doing."

3. See various works by Das Gupta, Hiriyanna, Radhakrishnan, Frauwallner, et al.

4. See my essay "Cross-Cultural Conversation: Its Scope and Aspiration," in Balslev (ed.), *Cross-Cultural Conversation*, pp. 15–27.

5. See p. 42 below. For thoughtful remarks on "intercultural comparisons," see Richard Rorty, "Philosophy, Literature, and Intercultural Comparisons: Heidegger, Kundera, and Dickens,"in *Essays on Heidegger and Others*, Volume 2 of his *Philosophical Papers* (Cambridge and New York: Cambridge University Press, 1991), reprinted on pp. 103–25 of this volume.

6. See Richard J. Bernstein, "The Hermeneutics of Crosscultural Understanding," in Balslev (ed.), *Cross-Cultural Conversation (Initiation)*, pp. 29–41, and Richard Rorty's review of Gerald J. Larson and Eliot Deutsch (eds.), *Interpreting Across Boundaries: New Essays in Comparative Philosophy* (Princeton: Princeton University Press, 1988), in *Philosophy East and West* 3/9 (1989): 332–37.

7. See my *A Study of Time in Indian Philosophy* (Wiesbaden: Otto Harrassowitz, 1983), pp. 140–50.

8. See my essay "Time and the Hindu Experience" in Anindita N.

Balslev and J. N. Mohanty (eds.), *Religion and Time* (New York and Leiden: E. J. Brill, 1993), pp. 163–81.

9. See Rorty's review of Larson and Deutsch (eds.), *Interpreting Across Boundaries* in *Philosophy East and West* 3/9 (1939): 332–37.

10. For Smart's and Staal's papers, see Larson and Deutsch (eds.), *Interpreting Across Boundaries*.

Letter 1

Charlottesville
May 6, 1990

Dear Dick,

Thank you very much for sending me a copy of your book *Contingency, Irony, and Solidarity* (Cambridge University Press, 1989). I am reading it as well as some of your papers carefully, making notes of the questions that I will eventually like to pose concerning the theme of "cultural otherness and philosophy," focusing especially on the encounter between India and the West. Whatever may have been the limitations of the Sixth East-West Philosophers' Conference held in Hawaii in August 1989, I would consider the endeavor laudable if it has succeeded in persuading the philosophers to be seriously concerned with questions that lie at the boundaries of the intellectual traditions of East and West. There are evidently various problems, but this is precisely what I am about to explore in and through this conversation with you.

As I have already told you, this is simply an initial sketch in an effort to understand what the issues really are and to grasp them as they spontaneously appear in the horizon, an attempt to catch a glimpse of in what way one should (or should not) prepare so that an authentic discourse may gradually emerge. This is perhaps itself a beginning (that is as we begin to converse), since the so-called crosscultural dialogue has essentially been so far an enterprise where one speaks *about* the other, and at best *to* the other, hardly ever it is witnessed as an open conversation. I am genuinely encouraged by the fact that you are willing to engage yourself in this question of crosscultural study (philosophy is only one aspect of this large and complex question). I think, this is one of the pressing issues of our time and must be attended to in all seriousness (that does not exclude a sense of humor and the comic). It has already become glaringly visible in the intellectual circles as the issue of "otherness."

On April 11, as I was getting ready to participate in the seminar on *The Cultural Other* organized at the Commonwealth Center of the University of Virginia, I could not help but thinking loudly about why this theme has become a recurrent topic for debates and discussions in our time? Does this reflect our need for achieving a higher level of critical self-understanding by placing ourselves in a larger context which today, more than ever, involves an encounter with the other? What do these frequent meetings tell us about our time? I would appreciate your comments.

It seems to me that this renewed vigor in the question of the self and the other, identity and difference, is very much due to a set of circumstances caused by technological advance which has turned strangers into neighbors. The situation then is this: technology has "killed the distance," the dialectical relationship between the self and the other, us and them, is no more perceived only as a purely abstract or theoretical concern. This is the academic setting in which the intense urge for a deeper understanding about what exactly constitutes the "otherness" of the other—in no matter which context, religious, social or political—is to be assessed. The academic zeal for this theme is prompted by the awareness that no meaningful communication with the other is feasible without some authentic information, not even a higher level of self-understanding is possible without it. This would imply that on practical, pragmatic ground alone (as well as, I believe, on a theoretical scrutiny) a theory (such as any expression of extreme relativism) which claims that we are prisoners of our respective conceptual worlds amongst which no communication is possible is bound to be rejected. The stand of extreme relativism is a purely theoretical construct, and has no cash value. Even on theoretical ground, it is self-defeating. The relevance of a philosophical stand in the contemporary situation would precisely be seen in its adequacy to explore the "otherness" in an authentic manner, taking note of its crosscultural dimension. There would be no harm, if the responses in this process get polarized.

I was emphasizing these questions simply in order to try to understand what the theme of "otherness" is telling us about our time. After all, the problems of one and the many, identity and difference are ancient themes of philosophy, in India and the West. Metaphysicians across cultural boundaries have for centuries wrestled with these questions disputing about which is primary, which is derived; which is real and which is appearance. The present concern with the theme of "otherness," a theme which is virtually appearing in a range of disciplines with all its acute tensions at the conceptual level, is an attempt to understand and to make sense of difference and pluralism. If at the point of departure one assumes that there is no possibility whatsoever to grasp the "otherness" of the other, one would have not much of a choice other than to describe the situation with a sense of comic and recite with Kipling: "All nice people like Us are We / And everybody else is They" (quoted in *They and We* by P. I. Rose [New York, 1964]).

Our awareness of "we" and "they" has become so sharpened that today in a multi-ethnic society we look with suspicion in a theory or in a practical policy-making what it is that is being compromised in the process of reorganization of whatever the issue is in question: is it our differences (which constitute our identity) that are overlooked at the cost of an abstract, unreal unity, or is it, as the anticommunitarians would say, that our common shared bonds are underplayed in order to highlight differences of all sorts, even those which are utterly irrelevant? Perhaps now more than ever we are intensely conscious of these issues or at least more articulate about them. (I recall that Professor Richard Bernstein also voiced some similar questions at the APA meeting in 1988.) Why so? Is there a threat of a loss of identity which our ancestors were unaware of that makes us so concerned with this theme?

Again, it is evident that although the theme of otherness is expressed in singular, it actually stands for a network of multiple, complex and complicated issues of various dimensions. In this adventure of a new, creative discourse our hope is that our self-understanding will grow along with our awareness of how stereotypes and clichés about the "otherness" of the other actually reflect back on our self-image. The factors that promote and thwart communication are gradually getting exposed to our critical gaze. I guess that ideas stemming from essentialism, relativism and various theories of interpretation, all provide strategies and competing paradigms for coping with this situation which is plural in every sense.

As I reflect on the question of otherness in the general context of the encounter of India and the West, what strikes me immediately is that our images of ourselves and views of otherness are not a set of unchanging thoughts and notions. The members of any given community are engaged in interpreting and making sense of these notions and this interpreting is a continuing, developing historical process (I elaborated some of these ideas in my paper presented in Hawaii). The perceptions do not remain static, but keep on changing from era to era. I wholeheartedly agree with you when you protest, as you did in Hawaii, against talking about the West not as "an ongoing, suspenseful adventure in which we are participating but rather as a structure which we can step back from, inspect at a distance" and then contrast "the West as a whole with the rest of the world as a whole."

Secondly, when we speak of the encounter between India and the West, we must note that none of these are names for cultural traditions that have monolithic structures. It is to be noticed that there is hardly one, homogeneous interpretation, one unique mode of self-understanding in any traditional frame, nor is there only a single, uniform perception of otherness, even if we confine ourselves to a selected time-period.

To give an example of how conflicting responses can coexist in a given society at the same time, consider the media-perceptions of the "otherness" of the other. During your frequent travels, I am sure that you have had plenty of occasions when you have noticed how responses vary, some completely agree with these media-perceptions and are influenced by them, whereas to some others these same projections appear as a blatant distortion of the "otherness" of the other, almost like a fiasco. It seems to me that not only there may be, but there actually simultaneously are several perceptions of the self and the other in any given traditional society. I am convinced that different groups in the Indian society have diverse and contrasting images of the West. Moreover, as I was arguing before, these images and perceptions do not remain static. They keep on changing and along with that our self-understanding also undergoes significant alterations. The concerns of one epoch may not remain relevant or even alive in another. I think that it is very important to take note of this heterogeneity within what is called one tradition. Evidently, to the extent that it is legitimate for us to refer to any cultural tradition as Indian or as Western, it must be possible to identify some broad and general characteristics of each. It remains, nevertheless, true that if one is to gain a rich, broad and adequate description of any tradition—whether Indian or Western—one should not downplay the tensions and oppositions that are inevitably present within each. In the wider context of encounter, these changes caused by the fusion of one with the other, of the old and the new, only bear witness to the fact that a tradition is a functioning tradition, that it is alive. I feel that the only thing that one has to be cautious about is whether perceptions of differences are getting so focused that they block conversation, whether the "otherness" of the other is projected as being so incommensurable that there is no more a legitimate basis for an exchange or a dialogue. That there will be room for a spectrum of views about these matters seems to me to be perfectly in order. That at different periods of history responses to "otherness" of the other culture vary can be clearly seen as one peruses the reactions of the prominent Indians, say from the nineteenth century to the last decade of the twentieth. No matter whose account one reads, whether Rammohan Roy's, Aurobindo's, or Nehru's, the picture of the nineteenth-century India is not a glorious one. It is invariably described as a stagnant, deteriorated state, when all creativity seems to have been in a subdued, repressed condition. These years of Indian history are often described as a dark period, albeit the darkness which occurs before the rising of the dawn: it was followed by the reassertion and the resurgence of the Indian spirit during what is frequently depicted as the Indian renaissance. This word, however, may not share exactly all the features that it has when applied to the European context, but some important common features may be detected. There is a rediscovery of the old roots and a revitalization of art, music, poetry, etc., in both. The peculiar characteristic of the Indian renaissance is not only a laborious search into the past of her own culture but also a conscious struggle in the face of an alien culture which it resented on various grounds and admired passionately on certain other grounds. The leaders who drew public attention and loyalty and who were caught in this process intellectually were in search of ways and means to cope with the "otherness" of the West. It was seen as an irreversible process. Aurobindo, for example, summarized in 1918 the impact of the European culture on India as: "It revived the dormant intellectual and critical impulse" and "awakened the desire of new creation."

As the locution of that time shows, "Western science and Indian spirituality" (there are also other pet phrases expressing the complementaries and the dichotomies) held a grip on the Indian mind: it could abandon neither of these. In fact, it is fascinating to read the chain of Indian thinkers from Rammohan Roy to Radhakrishnan, and notice how they have expressed their responses to the West. We might examine some of them at a later time.

What is of immediate interest, however, is to attend to the responses that an exposure to Western thought has provoked and is still provoking from philosophers in India. I think that this provides us with a glaring example of how the state of an academic discipline is tied to the factors which influence the over-all cultural history of India. At the beginning the response to Western thought could be seen in the ensuing of a host of "comparative studies." The story is intriguing. At this time, however, I would only like to observe that whatever the limitations and drawbacks of such studies, they did express a genuine philosophical need (whatever other motivations there might have otherwise been) which refuses to limit itself within a single culture. The value of this endeavor may itself be questioned and, as a matter of fact, has been questioned. Over the years the Indian response to Western thought can be seen as gradually shifting away from that. What is also interesting to note is that the Indians never shared the extreme views of such cultural relativists who claim that divergent intellectual histories lead to closed conceptual worlds amongst which no communication is possible. Anyhow, the enthusiasm for comparative studies has lessened. Perhaps it gradually turned out to be an intellectually tedious process that provoked doubts about its values. It is possible that in the history of the meeting of minds this was an inevitable phase that now needs to be transcended. It is felt that a mere comparativist cannot do creative philosophy. The Indian philosopher recognizes more than ever that whatever socio-political circumstances were responsible for the introduction of Western thought to the Indian mind, today it is accepted as a part of the Indian experience that can no more be expelled. The Indian philosopher today, perhaps, does not find it sufficient to relate to Western thought merely as an other but seeks to seize it in an authentic creative manner. He or she realizes that while a genuine involvement with the sources of Indian thought, its concerns, its analytical tools are essential for creative advancement of the tradition, it is not necessary to close off the possibilities of interpretation beyond the tradition's already achieved self-understanding. In this process the Indian philosopher also notes that the mainstream Western philosophy has not made much effort to understand and appropriate Indian thinking into its own texture. Some of the attempts to relate to the East on the part of the Western philosophers have precisely therefore been of the genre where the East is seen as a "redemptive force" or as bankrupt so far as philosophy is concerned. There have been some interesting discussions about this in recent times.

Now that the Hawaii conference is behind us, let me try to derive some wisdom from the past experience. Before I proceed, may I ask you what you exactly had in mind when you said at the Commonwealth Center in conversation with J. Ree in the fall of 1989 that at the Sixth East-West Philosophers' Conference in Hawaii (August, 1989) "the East did not meet the West"? What did you expect to happen? In what ways did the meeting not live up to that expectation? I ask this not in order to get your criticism of the past conference, which we all enjoyed and appreciated, but because I think that as you begin to articulate we will have some indications of what needs to be done in order to have a more fruitful conference in future. These glimpses, which usually appear in hindsight (and which conference is ever completely satisfying?), may provide us with some interesting clues which could be incorporated into the next meeting. I hope that it will take place in India and that it will be followed by a series of other conferences devoted to the same or similar theme over the years.

I will now begin by recalling some of the comments and observations which you made in your paper, presented in Hawaii, entitled "Philosophers, Novelists, and Intercultural Comparisons." Here you have pointed out that essentialism has not been fruitful as "applied to human affairs, in areas such as history, sociology and anthropology" and you have noted: "Despite growing recognition that the essentialistic habits of thought which pay off in the natural sciences do not assist moral and political reflection, we Western philosophers still show a distressing tendency to essentialism when we offer intercultural comparisons." You have also made the very important claim: "A society which took its moral vocabulary from novels rather than from ontico-theological or ontico-moral treatises would not ask itself questions about human nature or about the point of human existence or the meaning of human life. Rather, it would ask itself what we can do so as to get along with each other, how we can arrange things so as to be comfortable with one another, how institutions can be changed so that everyone to be understood has a better chance of being gratified."

If an essentialistic approach is, as you say, an "easy way out of the problem of intercultural comparison," how do you conceive a more adequate and fruitful approach? I recall in this connection that, just after the presentation of your truly stimulating paper in Hawaii, I asked you in the context of your above comments: "If comparative philosophy in making intercultural comparisons has exhibited essentialistic characteristics and thus far has failed, how do you envisage a program for philosophy as narrative for promoting such pragmatic virtues as tolerance for diversity, 'comfortable togetherness'—virtues you seem to endorse?" Now that there is more time I would like to dwell on some of the different ideas that you have put across. I do not see how you can do with simply not having a program (as far as I can recall you said that in your reply) and yet make a claim about which are the right questions to ask and which are not. From your observations, it seems to me that you have some insights at the level of theory, just as you have a practical concern, in recommending freedom and equality as some of the "West's most important legacy." You also record with approval that in its recent history the West has shown an "increased ability to tolerate diversity."

I hope that you will indicate one or two examples of essentialistic intercultural comparisons and show us precisely in what sense it is unfruitful and what is the way out. No one, as far as I can foresee, will question the pertinence of the virtues you recommend. There is, however, demand that values which are recommended must be shown to be realizable and hence there must be a program to cope with this demand both on the theoretical and the practical level.

Again, although I agree with you that the task of comparative philosophy does not end with the sorting out of "only our counterparts, those with tastes similar to our own," I do not quite see what is lost even if we keep on discovering what you describe as "the adaptations of a single transcultural character-type to different environments." Why can we also not consider the latter as an important part of the crosscultural adventure, as stumbling upon something where our stereotyped expectations of finding a pristine otherness/difference gets a jolt and we see some of "our" culture-types as indistinguishable from "theirs"—an experience where the distinction of "we" and "they" is in jeopardy? In other words, even if we grant that differences are what is really interesting, to rule out perceptions of similarity may also inflate our sense of distinctness or, to put it more strongly, our desperate need to save our sense of uniqueness beyond a point that can be accepted in good faith. To repeat it once more, I have no doubt that a keen awareness of conceptual distinctions that various intellectual traditions provide us is immensely valuable but caution must be exercised to see that the zeal for finding differences in the area of crosscultural studies does not get out of proportion as this can eventually lead to a distorted image of the "otherness" of the other culture. Later on I will give you one such example that I encountered in my work on the theme of time in an intercultural context.

Now, I would like to ask you a few questions and request you to elaborate on certain others pertaining to the much-discussed topic: Heidegger and the destiny of philosophy in the West as well as his observations about the East.

I will not try to organize the order of questions at this point but simply place them before you and return to this topic again adding still other queries.

It will be illuminating for us if you will kindly give a summary of your reading of the following comments of Heidegger: "That the thinking of the future is no longer philosophy, because it aims at thinking on a level deeper than metaphysics, which term also means the same"; "With the end of philosophy, thinking itself does not also come to an end but passes over to another beginning."

You have observed in your Hawaii paper that whereas for Kundera the Western adventure is open-ended, for Heidegger the West has "exhausted its possibilities." This you attribute to the inherent essentialistic structure of Heidegger's thinking. Would you please elaborate on this and show how this is related to a turning to the East—as something which is "wholly other" to the West? And what is wrong with this attitude?

You have obviously resented the observation made by Graham Parkes (ed., *Heidegger and Asian Thought*, [Honolulu, 1987]) where he writes:

> Heidegger's claim to be the first Western thinker to have overcome the tradition should be taken more seriously if his thought can be brought to resonate deeply with ideas that arose in totally foreign cultural milieu, couched in more or less alien languages, over two millennia ago.

You have reacted to it, as I find in the footnote of your paper, by saying that this "resonance can also be taken as a sign of regression rather than of transcendence—as a way of returning to the womb rather than a way of overcoming." Please elaborate.

At the end, I will also like to bring to your attention some comments of an Indian Heideggerian (perhaps you know his work on Heidegger), J. L. Mehta, to invite your own comment on them. In a paper entitled "Heidegger and the Comparison of Indian and Western Philosophy" (in *Philosophy and Religion* [Delhi: The Indian Council of Philosophical Research and Munshiram

Manoharlal Publishers, 1990], pp. 11ff) he has observed that from the scholarly point of view:

> The basic presupposition of the comparative enterprise would seem to be a history of Indian philosophy, in all the detail and scholarly refinement which the use of Western methods of philological and historical research makes possible. Only fragments of such a history are as yet available, and we in India can take further steps in this direction only when we shed the deep-seated notion that in the field of philosophy the historian's job is less philosophical than that of the systematic thinker and the dialectician, when we take a stance in the present and possess the detachment of inquiry which enables historical questions to be raised and requires that they be answered. We ask historical questions and seek to understand our tradition in its particularity when, from the perspective of a novel present, we experience a sense of remoteness from it, but also the urgency of a dialogue with it. The Indian philosophical tradition, like the Western, has been sustained by this dialectic of remoteness and creative appropriation all through its history, besides exhibiting the historical working out of the 'logic' inherent in different positions and systems; but by the rise of historical consciousness in the last hundred years must itself now be seen as marking a novel break in that tradition, demanding, a radically new kind of relationship to it, a new way of appropriating it, and thus breaking away from the hold of what is dead in it and yet being nourished by it.
>
> As a thinker of 'Being' and of 'Time,' Heidegger exhibits three integrally related features from which the Orient can learn: (1) a full awareness of historicity of understanding and thinking, even while pushing forward in the attempt to transcend it; (2) an intense consciousness of the intellectual and spiritual newness of the present, leading him to pose new questions to his own philosophical tradition, and thus to see, more vividly than even Hegel, its precise relation and relevance to the present as it has been molded by that tradition; and finally, (3) the radicality of the questioning with which he has confronted the Western tradition of metaphysical thinking, not with the intent to reject it, as is sometimes asserted, but as the only appropriate way in which we today are called upon to renew ourselves, as thinkers in a time of need, through an active and dedicated grappling with tradition.
>
> To take only the first as an example, it is well-known how a great deal of Heidegger's wrestling with 'the question of Being' is bound

up with 'what is' at present, here and now, with the way Western man is taken up in a technological mode of being and of being related to all that is, which for him is an extremity of spiritual impoverishment, a time of utter need and darkness in which man has ceased even to be aware of this need. The essence of the technological, according to Heidegger, is not itself technological, but is rooted in a destiny of Being (*Seinsgeschick*) of which the 'metaphysical' tradition of the West, beginning with Plato and culminating in the nihilism of Nietzsche, is an expression in the sphere of thought. The question of Being, as he raises it, amounts at the same time to a quest for a way of thought that can redeem our humanity by overcoming the 'oblivion way of Being' and so enable us to break the omnipotence of technology and live in the world as truly our home. . . . Further, he is also aware of the fact that the 'technification' of life originating in the West has enveloped, or threatens to envelop, the whole world. This strange destiny in which the whole world is caught up is described by him as the consuming Europeanization of the Earth, confirming in a sense Hegel's claim about the destiny of the West. For, to the extent that other cultures adopt the science and technology of the West, they also have a share in that 'history of Being' that progressive withdrawal of Being from man, which is the way Being and man have been related during the course and career of Western metaphysical thought, constituting its inner logic and hidden history.

It is this perverse 'triumph' of the West and in consequence the spiritual situation of not merely Western man but of men of all cultures and traditions today that forms the basic challenge to Heidegger's thinking, prompting him to attend a new beginning of thought, and to seek a way of thinking that is no longer parochial, moving within the charmed circle of concepts originating in the Western tradition, but planetary, as he calls it, beyond Orient and Occident, and for the first time truly world-historical.

Your comments on this will be most welcome.

The role of philosophy in relation to a culture as a whole needs to be closely looked into as the "ascetic priests" are taken seriously everywhere. Why have they been hailed across boundaries? Are they the pioneer architects of cultures? Can any culture really do without them? To whom then we shall turn to learn what's really wrong with us? Who will tell us, as in the context of the West you do, that it has turned into a sexist, racist and imperialist culture? The novelist? Why then, as you write, it is "among the philosophers of the West that Western self-hatred is most prevalent"? (It will be interesting to get some examples of that.) If this again, as you insist, is an attitude which belongs to the "annals of ascetic priesthood," what is the way out? It seems to me that the situation which you describe is something like this: one really does not want to go back on the diagnosis regarding the state of psyche in which one is but nevertheless resents an encounter with an ascetic priest (the philosopher) as it is no more *a la mode*, one would rather talk to a secular analyst (the novelist). In other words, the revolt is against an institution whose function cannot be denied but has to be demolished (in the name of what?), hence must be performed by another.

It is very likely that I am misinterpreting your stand. It is precisely in order to avoid such embarrassing situation that the prevalent custom in the area of "dialogue" is to speak *to* the other or *about* the other and never *with* the other—in which case most of the time the encounter with the other remains some sort of a fantasy, one hears only one's own voice. I am happy to take the risk as years of exposure alternatively to the East and the West has taught me that nothing can substitute for a conversation; it leads one along unpredictable lines where a new story presses for attention. So, please protest wherever my interpretation does not tally with your self-understanding.

I intend to continue but for the moment must rush this to you in order to get the conversation started.

With best wishes and regards,

Sincerely,
Anindita N. Balslev

Letter 2

Santa Cruz, California
August 1, 1990

Dear Anindita,

Let me begin replying to your thoughtful letter of May 6 by taking up the notion of "otherness." It is true that, as you say, "the problems of the one and the many, of identity and difference, are ancient themes of philosophy." But I doubt that philosophical discussions of these matters bear on the otherness which separates groups of people, and historical traditions, from one another.

The philosophical discussions have largely been about the rather artificial problem of understanding how the same, self-identical, thing could have many predicates, or about the equally artificial problem of which relations which a thing bears to other things could be taken away while maintaining the thing's self-identity. I call these problems artificial because they arise only if one has a doctrine of real essence if one does not, as I would, adopt the nominalist solution of saying that self-identity is a function of human interests.

This nominalism is part of my over-all pragmatist outlook. We pragmatists hope to dissolve traditional philosophical problems by viewing them as disguised forms of practical problems. Our slogan is that if it doesn't make a difference to what we do, it makes no difference at all. So we see every thing as simply a nexus of relations, in the sense in which a number is simply a nexus of relations to other numbers. We regard the question of which of these relations are internal to the thing (which could not be taken away while maintaining the thing's self-identity) as boiling down to the question "At what point would it be more convenient to stop using the same name or description, and to start using another one for identificatory purposes?"

Because of my nominalism and pragmatism, I am reluctant to speak, as you do, of "exploring the 'otherness' [between cultures or traditions] in an authentic manner." I would prefer to speak of the practical need of the members of an interdependent global society to get in touch with each other—figure out why the other is saying the strange things he or she does. I quite agree that we can set aside the claim that "we are prisoners of our respective conceptual worlds" on pragmatic grounds alone. A concept, on my nominalist view, is simply the use of a word. We can understand why people use other words than we do by noting the different environments in which each of us has developed languages—developed tools for coping with the different practical problems which their environments (natural and social) present. I do not see that questions about authenticity arise in regard to the manner in which we pursue our inquiries into those environments and those problems.

But perhaps by "authentic manner" here you simply mean is a "non-reductive manner"—one which does not assume that the other's words can be straightforwardly translated into words which we use. In that case, I quite agree with you. As we have learned from Kuhn and Davidson, the learnability of a language does not entail that sentences in it can be paired off in any straightforward way with sentences in another language. But this lack of pairability is not really very important; if the possibility of going bilingual exists, then this lack is merely a technical inconvenience. Davidson has, I think, given us good reason to believe that there is no such thing as an unlearnable language, so the possibility of bilingualism is always open, though difficult to realize in practice.

You raise the question of whether it may be a "threat of a loss of identity which our ancestors were unaware of" that makes us so concerned with "otherness" today. I am inclined to say that there are two factors which explain this concern. The first is just the fact you mention earlier— that technological civilization, and particularly developments in communication and transportation, make it impossible for us to ignore the existence of others in a way that was possible to our ancestors. But the second is just the love of the exotic—a love which has become an important feature of Western high culture since Herder, Humboldt, and the Romantics.

This love of the exotic—the taste for new ways of speaking and acting—has produced some bad results (those diagnosed in Edward Said's *Orientalism* for example) but on the whole it has been a progressive element in Western culture. For the Romantic idea that experience is wider than we have yet imagined (translated by us nominalists into the claim that there are not-readily-translatable languages to be learned) has helped the West stay alive to the idea that it doesn't know it all, and to the possibility that its own languages, and its own social practices, are relatively primitive. Romanticism has been linked with historicism, and so has produced the common Western assumption that our descendants will, with luck, speak a richer and more interesting language than the one we speak. In this Hegelian-Deweyan mood, we are not so much fearing to lose our identity as *hoping* to lose it. To my mind, the best and most hopeful element in the high culture of the West is the Romantic desire to acquire ever new identities— not to get stuck with the one you started with.

By "exotic," in this context, I do not just mean "characteristic of different lands," but rather "sufficiently different from what one is accustomed to force one to speak differently, to use different terms in characterizing oneself." So a new Western poet or painter can be as exotic, for the West, as an old Eastern poet or philosopher. The quest for the exotic is just the attempt to enlarge one's imagination. The Romantic-historicist notion of spiritual progress is not centered around the idea of understanding better and better something which is waiting out there to be understood, but rather around the idea of creating a larger, freer, self. The emphasis thus falls not on getting an "authentic" understanding of an old tradition or a new artistic movement but simply on finding something in that tradition or that movement which one can use for purposes of self-enlargement. More broadly, the emphasis falls less on knowing than on imagining, more on freeing oneself up than on getting something right.

Against this background, let me turn to your question about

how I can make do "with simply not having a program." You suggest that I ought to have some theoretical justification for the claim that freedom and equality are "the West's most important legacy," the things in the West which should be of most interest to inhabitants of non-Western cultures.

I do not have any philosophical backup for this claim, and do not feel the need of any. The claim is little more than a hunch that the way in which the recent West differs most interestingly from other cultures that have existed is in the utopian social aspirations which it has developed. The German historian of ideas Hans Blumenberg has suggested that at some point in the process of Europe's becoming "modern" the Europeans shifted from thinking of their relation to something ahistorical (God, or the Truth, or the order of the Universe) to thinking in terms of their relation to their descendants. On Blumenberg's view, their sense of what mattered most shifted from an atemporal object to a temporal one—the future state of humanity.

This shift was, it seems to me, partially the cause and partially the effect of the hope that science and technology might transform the conditions of human existence—transform them in such a way that hierarchical distributions of wealth and power might no longer be necessary for the functioning of society. This egalitarian hope flowed together, in the history of modern Europe, with the romantic hope that human beings might become larger, freer, richer beings than they had been in past ages. Taken together, they produce the idea that human beings can, without divine assistance, become new beings. They can do so simply by bringing about the leisure and wealth necessary for a fully egalitarian society—one in which basic needs are so well satisfied that individual differences of talent and opportunity do not arouse the sort of jealousy and resentment which has made previous history a struggle between haves and have-nots.

To sum up this hunch about what the West has been best at: the modern West has created a culture of social hope, as opposed to a culture of endurance. By a culture of endurance, I mean one in which there is a consensus that the conditions of human life are and always will be frustrating and difficult, and the consequent assumption that either a religious affiliation with a non-human power, or a philosophical acceptance of the eternal order of things, is required to make life bearable. The high culture of a peaceable society which does not have a future utopia to work for will center around priests or stoical sages. By contrast, the high culture of a society permeated by utopian hope will center around suggestions for drastic change in the way things are done—it will be a culture of permanent revolution.

I doubt that there is any way to show that the values of such a culture of hope can, as you put it, "be shown to be reliable." For it is a culture of experimentation, and nothing guarantees that the experiments will succeed. Technology may cause environmental catastrophe. It may also make possible the use of a secret police to insure the perpetual rule of a selfish oligarchy; this is the pattern we saw in the U.S.S.R. before Gorbachev came out of nowhere to change everything. Ever since the initial hopes raised by the French Revolution were dashed by the *sans-culottes'* Terror, the unreliability and riskiness of social experimentation has been clear.

Attempts have been made (notably by Marx and the Marxists) to combine a culture of hope with philosophical guarantees of reliability. These attempts consist in treating History as an object of inquiry, analogous to God or Nature. To my mind, any such attempt is a mistake, a misguided effort to keep something like knowledge-as-contemplation alive in a culture which has realized that theory is useful only insofar as it guides or changes practice. Philosophies of history which attempt to discern underlying patterns are, in effect, insisting that History is just more Nature— that humanity is not recreating itself, but merely acting out a role written for it by something non-human. Dewey was, I think, right in recognizing that one could usefully tell stories about the course of *past* history, but that one had to stop short at the present—that the future is a matter of hope and luck rather than of knowledge.

Heidegger seems to me an example of a Western thinker who, unlike Dewey, was unable to resist the temptation to claim a knowledge of the future. His discussions of technology are forecasts of an endlessly spreading desert, a world in which human happiness, and perhaps even human equality, are attained at the cost of losing touch with Being. In his use, the term "Being" becomes a name for everything most worth being in touch with. So his forecast of what will happen if we do not find some new postmetaphysical way of Thinking is a forecast of disaster. This forecast seems to me as bad as the Marxists' forecast of the inevitable triumph of the proletariat and of a communist society— not because either forecast is known to be inaccurate but because nothing could be adequate evidence for either. Marx hoped for, and Heidegger dreaded, what Mehta calls (in the passage you cite) "the consuming Europeanization of the Earth." I myself have no better scenario to write to spell out my hopes for the future than such Europeanization. But I would not want to justify this scenario by appeal to philosophical principles, or by any other sort of claim to knowledge.

I quite agree with Mehta that Heidegger has helped us develop an increased awareness of the historicity of understanding, but I am less sure that he has helped us to "an intense consciousness of the intellectual and spiritual newness of the present." This is because what seems to me new about the recent European past is not the increased pragmatism of high culture—what Heidegger thinks of as its nihilism, its deification of instrumental reason—but rather the increased freedom which has become possible for previously oppressed groups (e.g., unskilled laborers, women). To my mind, Heidegger neglects political newness for spiritual newness, and sees the political as merely a pallid reflection of the spiritual. He is unable to consider the possibility that social hope— hope for greater equality and less hierarchy—itself has spiritual significance. To put it another way, he tells a story about the modern newness which is confined to the newness of Nietzschean pragmatism in the history of philosophy. He acts as if an understanding of Nietzsche were automatically an understanding of modernity, of modern Europe.

As I see the matter, the pragmatism common to Nietzsche and to Dewey is a good thing, but only because it clears away some outdated philosophical assumptions. These assumptions are those left over from the days when the West had a culture of endurance rather than one of hope—a culture in which knowledge was assumed to be more important than imagination, finding more important than making. Pragmatism is useful for getting such assumptions out of the path of social progress, but pragmatism is not of the essence of the modern age, for pragmatism is merely a philosophical doctrine, and philosophical doctrines are not basic to historical epochs.

I am dubious about Mehta's claim—the claim which ends the passage from him which you cite—that Heidegger's "new beginning" is "planetary, beyond Orient and Occident, and for the first time truly world-historical." Certainly Heidegger wanted to get beyond "merely Western" assumptions, but equally certainly all he managed to do was to react against Western assumptions, and to hope that the West was not humanity's (or, in his terms, Being's) last word. I do not see why a highly specific and local reaction against highly specific and local conditions should claim planetary or world-historical significance. Perhaps Mehta's view will turn out to be justified; for all I know, the planetary civilization of the future will find inspiration in Heidegger and view his reaction against Nietzsche as a decisive turning-point. I certainly cannot prove the contrary, but I should be very surprised if the area of Heidegger's expertise—the canonical texts of Western philosophy—actually had the significance for humanity as a whole which Heidegger attributed to it.

In my "Philosophers, Novelists, and Intercultural Comparisons" paper (the one I read in Hawaii) I admitted that ascetic priests may well be indispensable to culture. It may be, as you suggest, that no culture will ever be able to do without them But it seems to me that your comments on what I said in that paper run together two functions—that of imaginatively attaining new perspectives and that of social protest against cruelty and injustice. In the West, the novelists and journalists seem to me to have taken over the latter function, though not the former. The West has been learning about its racism, its sexism and its imperialism not from philosophers, but from people who give us detailed accounts of what these social vices have done to individual human lives. As I see it, social protest is not a matter of what you call "diagnosis regarding the state of the psyche" but rather of calling attention to the effects of injustice on the victims. That is a distinct function from the one I attributed to the ascetic priests—speaking in new tongues, throwing out fresh metaphors, opening up new imaginative possibilities. Dickens did not do any of the latter things, but he did manage to make injustice and cruelty more visible than it had been previously.

Let me conclude this letter by saying something in response to your request for clarification of my remark that at the Hawaii conference we both attended "the East did not meet the West." Certainly East met West with considerable profit, but what I felt did not happen was that the philosophers from the West and those from the East found common options to discuss, options which were, for both, what William James called "live, immediate and forced." I suppose what I am really getting at is that the conference did not give me a sense of what the really hard choices confronting Eastern intellectuals of the present day are. Nor, I suspect, did my Eastern colleagues have much of a sense of the choices confronting their Western counterparts. I did not get the sense I hoped to attain of what it felt like to be an intellectual in a country whose native traditions have little to do with the Western hopes of a freer and more equal future generation. It seems to me that this hope is so basic to so much of Western philosophy since Hegel, that it is hard to get a sense of Eastern reactions to contemporary Western philosophical thought without having a sense of their reactions to current attempts to implement this hope. My hunch is that this sense might have been easier to attain if the participants in the conference had discussed philosophy less and politics (and perhaps novels) more.

With all good wishes,
Dick R.

Letter 3

Dear Dick,

In continuation of my letter of May 6, I wonder how you would respond to the view that depicting the novelist as the key spokesman of our time does not necessarily imply a rejection of philosophical thinking but that it rather reflects a move which can be described as a form of "genre mixing," an idea to which I will return shortly.

Moreover, a dialogue may be a very adequate and fruitful medium for conveying a philosophical message and, as a matter of fact, has been an ancient practice both in India and Greece. I do not see any difficulty in fantasizing that instead of an official spokesman of philosophy who appears, so to speak, in a well recognized uniform, now a character from a play or a novel will ask the questions, another will forward answers and still another will repudiate and reformulate the questions that today we describe as philosophical inquiry. I have, however, great difficulty in imagining that human beings will ever succeed in suppressing the source from which the torrent of questions have emerged in the past and are still emerging. After all, the conversation that is called philosophy, even in its very early days, has been in the form of questions and answers. Some of the issues which in later days of Indian thought became favorite topics for intellectual battle can be traced back to such exchanges between teacher and pupil, husband and wife, or father and son—as recorded in the Upanishads, and other less authoritative but influential sources. A change of format is not the end of a certain genre of discourse; it may have other ways and other modes of self-expression. Myths, dialogues, debates have all been found to be suitable medium for carrying out such a project. It is perhaps so, simply because there are many ways of looking at philosophy.

When there is a marriage between philosophy and drama or novel, what often dominates the narrative is the actual input of the ideas that guide the decisions, choices and the course of actions of the different characters. Certainly during my graduate days in Paris, especially while reading Sartre, I found that some of the characters of his plays and novels are superb existentialists. In other words, novels and plays in some ways served better, the cause of Sartre's philosophy than his official philosophical treatises, such as *Being and Nothingness* and others, (and certainly more effectively spread the message to many more readers).

A mixing of genres, perhaps gives the author the freedom to cross the rigidity of the boundaries, and may be recognized as a novel and effective medium for the philosopher of tomorrow.

As you know, Clifford Geertz has spoken eloquently about "blurred genres" as a phenomenon which is widespread today ("Blurred Genres: The Refiguration of Social Thought," in *The American Scholar* 49 [1980]):

> It is difficult to label either authors (What is Foucault—historian, philosopher, political theorist? What is Thomas Kuhn—historian, philosopher, sociologist of knowledge?) or to classify works (What is George Steiner's *After Babel*—linguistics, criticism, cultural history? What is William Gass's *On Being Blue*—treatise, causerie, apologetic?). And thus it is more than a matter of odd sports and occasional curiosities, or of the admitted fact that the innovative is, by definition, hard to categorize. It is a phenomenon general enough to suggest that what we are seeing is not just another redrawing of the cultural map—the moving of a few disputed borders, the marking of some more picturesque mountain lakes but an alteration of the principles of mapping. Something is happening to the way we think about the way we think.

What do you think is happening? Is it really an event of any major significance? Since Geertz's paper came out, a decade has passed. Are you convinced that the boundaries of disciplines will shift to a point where the global "cultural map" will begin to look different, more than a mere minor adaptation here and there? If so, it is bound to have a profound impact on crosscultural studies. It seems to me to be so since the criteria for determining the "otherness" of the other cultures are systematically supplied by the various disciplines which study cultures such as Geertz's own discipline—anthropology.

Perhaps this is a question which belongs to that domain which deals with what is called the power politics of knowledge. It is evident to anyone that the various disciplines have a deep influence on and a complex relation with the structures of power and value around which the society at large organizes its life. It can also be seen the other way round, by putting it in terms of the existing power structures that sustain and support the institutions which cultivate these disciplines and disseminate knowledge accordingly. Thus, self-criticism on the part of such disciplines— which avowedly claim it to be their business to study cultures— should be encouraged if new descriptions/interpretations are at all to emerge. These descriptions which are open as well as camouflaged interpretations of "we" and "they" are not only expressions of the sort of remote from life, pure and simple theoretical sophistications but embody built-in attitudes and assumptions that eventually come to play a decisive role in the choices and decisions we make and thereby influence the course of our actions. In a literate society, the "common" man, even if he has not acquired all the theoretical sophistications, has been trained in institutions which have made sure that he is equipped with images of the self and the other, based on a so-called objective study, that shape his attitudes and actions (of which he may not be always aware) in the transactions of his daily life. Today, therefore, there is a demand for an analytical and critical scrutiny of the various disciplines, which is prompted by the need for a fresh self-understanding and a review of alterity. Recall Edward W. Said's observations ("Secular Criticism," in *Critical Theory Since 1965*, ed. by Adams and Searle [1986], p. 612):

> The entire history of nineteenth-century European thought is filled with such discriminations as these, made between what is fitting for us and what is fitting for them, the former designated as inside, in place common, belonging, in a word *above*, the latter, who are

designated as outside, excluded, aberrant, inferior, in a word *below*. From these distinctions, which were given their hegemony by the culture, no one could be free, not even Marx—as a reading of his articles on India and the Orient will immediately reveal . . . they are to be found everywhere in such subjects and quasi-subjects as linguistics, history, race theory, philosophy, anthropology and even biology.

In other words, the task that is set by our critical consciousness is not to let go the official, standard interpretative practices of these disciplines unquestioned but to unmask their professed neutrality. With the growth of a keen critical awareness regarding the importance of learning "to think globally," it seems to me, the demand for an authentic crosscultural study will have to be seriously taken. It will, most likely, shake the existing frames of disciplines for which the boundaries of cultures have been the object of study. There is an acute need for new interpretive strategies. This will have a direct bearing on the boundaries that disciplines so far have demarcated in the way they have studied cultures. Questions will arise such as, how does one define the boundary today? In what way is it different from that of yesterday—when the stories of "otherness" of the other cultures were a part of the repertoire of humanities' travelers' tales? If there is no significant alteration in these notions, what then is that "distance" that technology supposedly has "killed"? What are the emerging perceptions regarding "the fusion of horizons" between cultures (to borrow an expression of Gadamer)? Is there resistance to change? If so, how does it express itself?

Some years ago I saw on the television, Margaret Mead suggesting that chairs should be instituted for professors studying the future since there are already many in the universities for those studying the past. I recall it as a relevant advice in this context. A search for a new paradigm, with the view to comprehend identity and difference in the broad and general area demarcated for crosscultural studies, has to be carried out in an inter-disciplinary context. Such a study has to deal with a cluster of problems which requires, no doubt, familiarity with the past records of our interpretive discourses and of our actions but it also calls for a sense for the future. To sense that change is inevitable even if it is not visible in any gigantic scale perhaps is more disturbing to the thinking mind than is generally admitted. To ask the relevant questions, let alone to answer them, requires imagination and skill—about how to draw from the past yet be forward looking. Recently questions have been raised about the rigidity and fluidity of the boundaries of disciplines, touching upon the issues of how freely one may move from one discipline to another covering a range of different but not unconnected areas of inquiry. Is it possible to guess the changing roles of disciplines in relation to the rest of the culture? Or, can one even predict the end of some disciplines (such as the end of philosophy, for example)? Let us hope that it is so that the time is ripe for something to happen. What we need, however, is a sense of direction. Where are those cosmopolitan thinkers who know how "to think globally" without demolishing the local differences? We need those who can perceive the encounter-situation as a possibility for greater self-enrichment in an unexpected manner, opening up unpredictable avenues of self-development. It of course also involves facing the tension between the self and the other, risking even the possibility of having to admit the oversights and blindness of one's own tradition.

To approach "cross cultures" as an intellectual adventure calls for a resolution to free ourselves (i.e. the participants) of the indoctrinations to which we have all been subjected. Surely, all this requires that the participants have more information. The alien cultural tradition, one has the impression, has been in the West very largely a subject of interest for the non-philosophers. The mainstream Western philosophy can hardly be said to have made much effort in that direction so far. It seems that there is a genuine need to have conferences and workshops devoted to this purpose. One of the questions which probably calls for attention at the outset concerns the very concept of philosophy—is it essentially a Greek concept? "Is there philosophy in Asia?" Docs *darśana* or *ānvīkṣikī* in the Sanskritic tradition correspond at all to what is called *philosophia* in the West?

It is also essential to probe into the age-old habits of contrasting the Indian and Western thought traditions, saying for example that Indian thought, as distinct from the Western, is spiritual, that it relies more on intuition than on intellect. I need not go into these here as I am sure that you have come across such a list of dichotomies over and over again. There is, however, little doubt in my mind that one of the major tasks that lie before the scholar involved in crosscultural studies is to identify and eventually unmask the stereotyped images that have vitiated intercultural understanding. Changing the world (as they say) involves, at least to a large extent, changing the construal of the "otherness" of the other, which will eventually alter the self-understanding of the participants as well. In any case, there can be hardly any doubt that something is bound to happen if the scholars across boundaries take genuine interest in such a project and are willing to seek novel strategies.

I myself became acutely aware of the problems of crosscultural studies in the course of working on the theme of time—a theme which has deservedly drawn the profound attention of the philosophers in the West especially during the last one hundred years. Along with my passionate interest in the development of the various ideas on time in the history of Western thinking, I went through the Sanskritic texts in search of distinct conceptual models of time that emerged in the history of Indian thought. I found that the philosophical situation in the Indian context was at serious variance with what I was given to believe, *viz.*, that time is not an issue of major importance in Indian thought, that time is generally considered to be illusory, that time is not linear but cyclic. The situation is, as is to be expected in a major thought tradition, a spectacular display of a wide range of contrasting and conflicting views. If some advocated a view of absolute time, others questioned this very idea. Again for some, time is discrete as opposed to continuous and so on and so forth. Being a central theme, these different views of time were woven into the texture of various schemes that know of a great variety of notions regarding being, becoming and non-being, space and causality.

For an understanding of the ancient Indian cosmological speculations, where one comes across the idea of repeated creation and dissolution, the theme of time comes to play an important role. The grand cosmological model that is widespread in the Indian conceptual world, is one where each world cycle is measured in astronomical terms (cf. my paper on "Cosmology and Hindu Thought," *Zygon* [March 1990]).

In an intercultural context, however, this vast panorama of Indian thought with all its variations and contrasts is often ignored and clichés such as that the Indian view of time is cyclic and other stereotyped ideas have been repeated endlessly. I will not go into the details here as I have discussed this question, at the risk of repeating myself, in various talks and papers as in *Time, Science and Society in China and the West*, ed. Fraser, Lawrence and Haber [Univ. of Massachusetts Press, 1986]). I became acutely aware of the pernicious implications and consequences of such apparently simple metaphorical descriptions which set up the thought traditions of the world almost as "diagrammatically opposed." Sometimes this is done in such a manner that to the participants of a given culture it seems more like a caricature, since it does not tally with their self-understanding. This has impact on various facets of crosscultural studies, as time is a theme which is intertwined with various aspects of the distinct history of our cultural traditions—covering the wide domains of mythology and religion, science and philosophy. Many perceptive culture historians, and concerned theologians who have attempted to classify and appraise the major views concerning time and history (cf. Arnold Toynbee, *A Study of History* [New York, 1972] and Paul Tillich, *The Protestant Era* [Chicago, 1948]) have been led astray by such facile generalizations.

The "bias towards overthematization" is undeniably glaring when one observes how the expressions of linear and cyclic time have come to designate distinct cultural experiences of time. As I have cited elsewhere, the observation made by an anthropologist, P. Kay, is relevant in this context:

> Time is perhaps the favorite thing anthropologists point to so as to exaggerate the exoticness of other people, they love to say things like 'time is this' for us but it is like that for the folk that I studied.

I take this as a specimen of self-criticism of a discipline—anthropology—regarding how it ascribes a sense of otherness to the culture which is the object of its study. It is indeed not a trivial observation. It should be questioned whether the experiences of

irreversibility and recurrence are emphasized in any such absolute and exclusive manner in any culture that such schematizations of cultural representation of time can be justified, even if one
insists—as does C. Geertz—that "the question isn't really whether
everybody has every thing . . . but rather the degree to which
things are elaborated and their power and force." (Having seen
the pernicious influence of these time-metaphors, one would
wish that Geertz paid more attention to what Kay was saying.)

It is indeed amazing to note how cycles and arrows gradually
cease to be simple time-metaphors and come to get associated
with such concepts as history, progress and even salvation. It also
becomes slowly apparent how the schematizations of time-repre-
sentations of various cultures express what Fabian in his *Time and
the Other* described as "denial of coevalness" to the other culture.

As one peruses the relevant literature, one sees that it is not at
all very unusual that the concept of time in one tradition is played
down as contrasted with another. Arnaldo Momigliano, in an
essay entitled "Time in Ancient Historiography" (in *Quarto Con-
tributo* [Rome, 1969]) observes: "In some cases they oppose Indo-
European to Semitic, in other cases Greek to Hebrew, in others
still Greek to Jewish-Christian or Christian alone." I keep repeating these citations over and over again as these are all warnings
which must be paid heed to by those interested in crosscultural
conversations. Unfortunately, to set up one tradition against another is nothing uncommon in schemes that are especially
worked out to aid crosscultural and interreligious dialogue. The
presuppositions of such schemes often go unnoticed and therefore their untenability is not detected. These cliches, evidently
block our perceptions by giving a simplistic picture of a tradition
or a culture.

As you may recall I presented some of these ideas in an
interdisciplinary symposium (1989) on the theme of *Time Metaphors: Cycles and Arrows*, which I organized with Professor H.
Kelly, then Dean of the Faculty of Arts and Sciences, University of
Virginia. This symposium was an attempt to review how cycles
and arrows as time metaphors appear in discourses in an inter-
disciplinary (such as biology, physics, cosmology, theology) context. Cycles and arrows, being major metaphors, appear and

reappear not only in our everyday discourse but take on, in the frame of specific disciplines, technical significance. Since time is a multidimensional issue, the early formulations of various traditions are of particular interest for the self-understanding of cultures. Recall St. Augustine's *City of God* where he polemicizes against a certain Greek view of "circular time" which is derived from a world view in which "during countless past ages, at very prolonged yet definite intervals, the same Plato, the same city and the same students had existed again and again." Augustine by repudiating this view of exact mechanical recurrence, not only of cosmological processes but also of individual destinies, puts in relief the Christian contribution to the religious interpretation of time. It seems to me that one of the vital problems in the area of crosscultural studies is to see how the interpretation of an "outsider" relates to the historical process of interpretation by the members of the community themselves, i.e. the "insiders." The problem of understanding then is this second level of interpretation. The important question is what would be the criterion for distinguishing an authentic interpretation by an outsider from an inauthentic one? One could just as well also ask whether the interpretations of the insiders are always authentic. It is evident that the distinction between an authentic and an inauthentic interpretation is not equivalent to the distinction between an outsider's and an insider's interpretation. What would be the pragmatist's solution to this? If one says that no matter whether the interpretation is the insider's or the outsider's, that interpretation alone is to be considered to be authentic which is really grounded in the historical consciousness of a tradition, in that case what new can at all emerge in the second level of interpretation? It is, however, certain that an outsider's interpretation cannot be deemed to be authentic if the community of the insiders find it not to tally with their own self-understanding. I am sure that you will have illuminating comments on these questions.

By the way, I saved your letter which you wrote to me after reading my paper presented at the symposium on time metaphors, precisely because I wished that you further elaborate your insightful comments on this issue. This seems to me to be a suitable occasion for requesting you to do so as it has direct relevance for our present exchange. With reference to my paper you wrote:

> I found it very illuminating indeed. . . . I thought your quote from Momigliano very apt, and I thought your material added a lot of force to the point he was making. My hunch is that if Kant hadn't called space and time "forms of sensibility" we would have heard much less from anthropologists and cultural historians than we have about different "experiences of time." The Kantian metaphors have had an extraordinarily wide-ranging and, on the whole, pernicious effect.

I look forward to reading your observations as time is a question in which my interest does not seem to fade, so any fresh insight pertaining to any aspect of this issue is welcome. The remarks that you make in your letter, it seems to me, when elaborated, will help to understand some interconnections between philosophy and other disciplines in the West that directly deal with crosscultural studies. It will be interesting to hear from you how you perceive the culture historian and the anthropologist operating, actually being influenced by the Kantian metaphor.

It will be also fascinating to see how you employ the idea of interpretation while describing the encounter situation in the context of the meeting of philosophical traditions (for the moment let us lay aside the issue whether philosophy is exclusively a Greek concept or not) stemming from diverse cultural soils. Here, that is, the sort of conference we are hoping for, the dialogue partners are our contemporaries, all of whom carry a heavy burden of the past without which they will be at a loss to locate themselves in a philosophical space. Do you agree with the theory of interpretation of Gadamer on all points when he writes that:

> Every encounter with tradition that takes place within historical consciousness involves the experience of the tension between the text and the present. The hermeneutic task consists in not covering up this tension by attempting a naive assimilation but consciously bringing it out. This is why it is part of the hermeneutic approach to project an historical horizon that is different from the horizon of the present. Historical consciousness is aware of its own otherness and hence distinguishes the horizon of tradition from its own. On

the other hand, it is itself, as we are trying to show, only something laid over a continuing tradition, and hence it immediately recombines what it has distinguished in order, in the unity of the historical horizon that it thus acquires, to become again one with itself (p. 273).

How would you read the significance when transposed in an intercultural context?

As I was saying earlier, perhaps there are many ways of looking at philosophy and the description of the encounter-situation will vary accordingly. I enjoyed reading when you write (*Consequences of Pragmatism*, The University of Minnesota Press [1982], pp. 91–92) that:

> Philosophy started off as a confused combination of the love of wisdom and the love of argument. . . . As philosophical thought changed and grew . . . both wisdom and argumentation became far more various than Plato dreamed. . . . Given the nineteenth-century complications. . . . One cannot even seek an essence for philosophy as an academic Fach (because one would first have to choose the country in whose universities' catalogs one was to look). The philosophers' own scholastic little definitions of "philosophy" are merely polemical devices— intended to exclude from the field of honor those whose pedigrees are unfamiliar. We can pick out the "philosophers" in the contemporary intellectual world only by noting who is commenting on a certain sequence of historical figures. All that "philosophy" as a name for a sector of culture means is "talk about Plato, Augustine, Descartes, Kant, Hegel, Frege, Russell . . . and that lot." Philosophy is best seen as a kind of writing. It is delimited, as is any literary genre, not by form or matter, but by tradition—a family romance involving, e.g., Father Parmenides, honest old Uncle Kant, and bad brother Derrida.

Will you grant that the very concept of philosophy is a generic concept? As a genre of thinking, as a kind of writing it may retain a well-recognizable character—and this is no transcultural abstraction—in the distinctly different expressions. How do we recognize art, music or literature in other cultures? If there is no question of making any special effort in obtaining any intercultural consensus about these which presupposes a transcultural "we," why treat philosophy as an expression which is restricted to any single culture?

There have been many myths about the East in the West and vice versa. As an example of a well-articulated description of how Eastern thought was assessed, consider the following lines which Husserl wrote in 1935 in his *Philosophy and the Crisis of Humanity*:

> Today we have a plethora of works about Indian philosophy, Chinese philosophy, etc., in which these are placed on a plane with Greek philosophy and are taken as merely different historical forms under one and the same idea of culture. Naturally, common features are not lacking. Nevertheless, one must not allow the merely morphologically general features to hide the intentional depths so that one becomes blind to the most essential differences of principle.

Husserl did not stop there but attempted to focus on these differences, voicing an opinion which is not grounded on any genuine acquaintance but rather a superficial characterization of Eastern thought. He points out:

> In both cases one may notice a world-encompassing interest that leads on both sides—thus also in Indian, Chinese, and similar 'philosophies'—to universal knowledge of the world, everywhere working itself out as a vocation-like life-interest, leading through understandable motivations to vocational communities in which the general results are propagated or develop from generation to generation. But only in the Greeks do we have a universal ('cosmological') life-interest in the essentially new form of a purely 'theoretical' attitude . . . and the corresponding, essentially new (community) of philosophies, of scientists (mathematicians, astronomers etc.). These are men who, not in isolation but with one another and for one another, i.e. in interpersonally bound communal work, strive for and bring about *theoria* and nothing but *theoria*.

It is indeed interesting that the intellectuals in the West usually do not seem to have much trouble in discerning Hindu mathematics as mathematics, or astronomy as astronomy, or grammar as grammar, or even poetry as poetry, why, I wonder, it is especially difficult to recognize any crosscultural experience and expression as philosophy.

You write in your review of a book (*Interpreting Across Bounda-*

ries: New Essays in Comparative Philosophy, ed. Gerald James Larson and Eliot Deutsch, Princeton, 1988) devoted to various aspects of comparative philosophy, that:

> The attempt to compare 'philosophies' either means comparing entire intellectual horizons—or it means comparing something much more narrow and specialized. What we in the West call 'philosophy' became what it is by successively distinguishing itself, self-consciously and insistently, from theology, natural science, and literature The sequence of intellectual history was very different in the various parts of Asia, so we may well wonder ... whether applying the term 'philosophy' to Asian books is more than an empty gesture, a stilted complement that creates more awkwardness than collegiality. Unless we fall in with what Ninian Smart calls "the imperial assumption that somehow there is a clearly well-defined place in our intellectual firmament for what is called philosophy," we shall have to grant Smart's claim that "modern Western philosophy has been the product of a number of cultural accidents, one of which is institutionalization of universities into a departmental structure." It is perfectly reasonable to ask, without condescension and in honest bewilderment, the question which forms the title of Staal's essay "Is There Philosophy in Asia?" For this is not the question "Is Asia intellectually mature?" but the question "Have Asians had any of the needs which have led Western universities to teach Seneca, Ockham, Hume, and Husserl in the same department?"

Perhaps what we need, more than any amount of sophisticated *a priori* arguments designed to inquire where there is philosophy and where it is nonexistent, is to find devices to make us familiar with each others' tradition—as you have said that like literature philosophy is not a matter of form or matter but that of a tradition. Any *a priori* argument (such as insisting on the differences in intellectual histories or others) need to be postponed until effort is made by professional philosophers to acquaint themselves with the intellectual traditions to which they have been hitherto closed, and in your case—if I may say so—until you "can sketch a dramatic narrative leading up to ourselves." "The story of the making of the modern mind" will then be even thousandfold richer.

I am very much inclined to think that the more the philosophers of different parts of the world will become familiar with each others' traditions, it will be seen that philosophers need not fear the vigilant guards waiting at the boundaries. In whatever way we may think of demarcating human thinking, we need not be put off by such geographical descriptions as German Idealism, American Pragmatism, or Indian Vedanta as designation of territories where only a native can have a proper access and others can contemplate only from outside. If there is an authentic urge today for the meeting of minds across boundaries, let us by all means seize upon this psychological factor as a saving grace.

The aim of such a conversation is not to obliterate differences, not by any means, but on the contrary to preserve them as they arouse in us "a renewed sense of wonder and novelty" (as Daya Krishna describes it).

On the theoretical level, however, there are problems to be faced and resolved. Even if there is no difficulty in granting that diversity is something immensely desirable, the idea of ethnocentrism needs to be carefully spelled out. Ethnocentrism, whether every author actually describes the phenomenon by that term or not, has found several prominent exponents in our days. Lévi-Strauss spoke strongly against UNESCO cosmopolitanism in his well-known work, *The Views from Afar*. He pointed out the importance of not "to confuse racism . . . with attitudes that are normal, even legitimate . . . and unavoidable." To advocate cosmopolitanism is not to deprive a culture of its right to be understood in its own terms and its need to resist other cultures from which it distinguishes itself. Some have argued, against this position, by pointing out that to support ethnocentrism may lead to abandon such aspirations of equality, liberty and fraternity on the part of all those cultures claiming a distinct identity and to foster the wish that one's cultural values alone should prevail. This latter position has a good possibility of being interpreted as a form of cultural imperialism in disguise.

This could be said, I would imagine, when you claim that "the pragmatist attempt to see the history of humanity as the history of the gradual replacement of force by persuasion, the gradual spread of certain virtues typical of the democratic West" . . . unless you disclose the steps of the argument why you think that these are commendable for the entire world? Which are, specifically, the virtues you have in mind? Even then, one may still find difficulties at the theoretical level of intercultural communication. If one follows the Deweyan idea and thinks of "rationality not as the application of criteria (as in a tribunal) but as the achievement of consensus (as in a town meeting)," how does a politically conscious intellectual make any recommendation when the "other" has not been present in the meeting? One may insist that in your frame there cannot be any sense for "we"—according to you the pragmatist who has "given up the Kantian idea of emancipation" there is no persistent "we," in the sense of a transhistorical metaphysical subject, in order to tell stories of progress. The only "we" we need is a local and a temporary one: "we" means something like "us twentieth-century Western social democratic intellectuals." At the level of theory what is exactly achieved? Despite the whole set of ideas—to renounce the idea of a transhistorical criterion of justice or the notion of a human nature or even insisting on persuasion rather than of force—the pragmatist seems to have aroused nothing but suspicion. This is obvious from the writings of your opponents (think of Taylor and others). What you describe to be your position—a form of "mild ethnocentrism"—has been seen by others as "secondary narcissism," as fascism, even as cultural imperialism.

If these sort of objections and questions are not infrequent, it only shows that you are widely read. If this is not a correct understanding of the pragmatist position that you hold, a direct response from you is needed. I know that you have answered to some of these charges raised by your opponents (as in "Cosmopolitanism Without Emancipation: A Reply to Lyotard" or in "Comments On Geertz's 'The Use of Diversity'"). It will be interesting, however, if you deal with these questions here, even if you cannot go into the detail, as these ideas have direct bearing on crosscultural studies, which is the principal concern of our conversation. I would also like to hear what your vision really is regarding the "future cosmopolitan society," what are the implications of the idea of the "ever more inclusive universal histories" for the non-Western world? After all, in your own admission the "we" refers to the "we twentieth-century Western social democratic intellectuals" and the vocabulary of this ethnic group is supposed to be "the best vocabulary the race has come up with so far."

The pragmatist utopia to build a cosmopolitan world society will be still suspected. It is just not enough to say: "The pragmatist drops the revolutionary rhetoric of emancipation and unmasking (shared by Voltaire, Julien Benda, and Edward Said) in favor of a reformist rhetoric about increased tolerance and decreased suffering." If you think that this observation and the ones from your opponents do not do justice to the pragmatist ideas that you are advocating, please say it (as loudly as you can).

I would really appreciate if you elaborate on the pragmatists' understanding of human solidarity. In your essay entitled "Postmodernist Bourgeois Liberalism" (*The Journal of Philosophy* [1983]: 583–84) you have summarized the basic attitudes that debates in contemporary social philosophy reflect. You describe

> . . . [a] three-cornered debate between Kantians (like John Rawls and Ronald Dworkin) who want to keep an ahistorical morality-prudence distinction as a buttress for the institutions and practices of the surviving democracies, those (like the post-Marxist philosophical left in Europe, Roberto Unger, and Alasdair MacIntyre) who want to abandon these institutions both because they presuppose a discredited philosophy and for other, more concrete, reasons, and those (like Michael Oakshott and John Dewey) who want to preserve the institutions while abandoning their traditional backup.

This is an intriguing picture. It will be interesting to know whether your "distrust of metanarratives" and your views on postmodernist bourgeois liberalism will undergo any change if one places this debate in a wider context than the contemporary West, in a crosscultural context, for example, which is the backdrop of this exchange. On a theoretical level how does one proceed to resolve intersocietal or intrasocietal tensions if the legitimacy of principles—moral and/or prudent—which govern our actions are entirely derived from the practices of the members of a given society. Let alone the differences between different groups or societies, even within the so-called same group there are controversies and disputes. To what does one appeal in the absence of a metanarrative which could, so to speak, provide with norms, rules (such as the notion of an ahistorical human nature, or a universal concept of rationality or something else), how does one cope with the question of any code of human behavior—while attempting to make a theory—and persuade anyone whose rules of the game are otherwise? On what basis, for example, can you recommend certain virtues of the democratic West to the entire world? Is there not an unrecognized assumption somewhere— because of which these pragmatic virtues are expected to benefit all across frontiers? If virtues, i.e., moral attitudes, were ethnocentric, rooted exclusively in the soil of particular cultures and traditions, how can one advocate (that is, in consistency with this theory) spreading the same virtues beyond the boundary of a given tradition or culture? How can one even condemn planned holocausts, famines that are designed and other similar events and practices (not easy to obtain a complete list of the variety and range of suffering that human beings inflict on those whom they call "others," as a token of their loyalty to their own group) which may even be regarded as perfectly legal in a given historical context? What is the substitute for a metanarrative? I see that I am back again to the same point where I was after I heard your paper at the East-West conference. Does the task of a theoretician end simply by denouncing the essentialistic story of human affairs? The pragmatist's wish and ability to unweave a theory creates a mood of suspense in the listener's mind who awaits an yet-untold story of philosophy, surely not its end, even if the story-teller wishes to stop there. The story of the end (in no matter whose version it is), so far as we have heard, is not convincing, it sounds more like as if philosophy lived ever after, although we do not know whether it did so happily or unhappily.

It will be interesting to hear what you think about such readings as sketched above. Perhaps your reading regarding the destiny of philosophy is much more complex than that. Is it possible to bring to the surface that which has remained unsaid about what you exactly wish to see as the destiny of philosophy? I was wondering about that while I was enjoying your description of the anti-theorists' unweaving of a theory. You suggested that:

We should stay on the lookout, when we survey other cultures, for the rise of new genres— genres which arise in reaction to, and as an alternative to, the attempt to theorize about human affairs. We are likely to get more interesting, and more practically useful, East-West comparisons if we supplement dialogues between our respective theoretical traditions with dialogues between our respective traditions of anti-theory. In particular, it would help us Western philosophers get our bearings in the East if we could identify some Eastern cultural traditions which made fun of Eastern philosophy. The kind of fun I have in mind is not the in-house kind which we philosophers make of one another . . . but the kind made by people who could not follow a philosophical argument if they tried, and have no wish to try.

It will be of course very enjoyable but I am afraid that even if the attacks on philosophy come from the quarter of the anti-theorists, their eventual impact will not be any more destructive or severe than the ones that come from professional philosophers—perhaps because weaving of theories is a preoccupation difficult to abandon, perhaps we can attempt to do so only at the risk of being inconsistent. Thus in the context of a theory of conversation between nations, especially with reference to the Vietnam War, when the belief-system of the American community is questioned by the American intellectuals themselves, one may imagine a situation where a child who is "found wandering in the woods, the remnant of a slaughtered nation whose temples have been razed and whose books have been burned." You write that "this is indeed a consequence, but it does not follow that she may be treated like an animal. For it is part of the tradition of our community that the human stranger from whom all dignity has been stripped is to be taken in, to be reclothed with dignity. This Jewish and Christian element in our tradition is gratefully invoked by freeloading atheists like myself." The question which still needs to be answered, in order to satisfy our quest for a theory, is whether this invoking of the Jewish and Christian element does not show the inadequacy of the postmodernist bourgeois liberalism to support such a course of action without a metanarrative (which dominates the Judeo-Christian conceptual world and in accordance with which it recommends and prohibits specific course of action? To emphasize this as part of "the tradition of our community" is only to admit that this "tradition" cannot be adequately expressed in a consistent ethnocentric telling.

I look forward to hearing from you.

With kind regards,
Anindita N. Balslev

Letter 4

Santa Cruz, California
August 12, 1990

Dear Anindita,

In the continuation of your earlier letter, you raise the question of whether novelists can be thought of as answering philosophical questions. You speak of "the source from which the torrent of [philosophical?] questions have emerged." You speak of philosophy as a "certain genre of discourse," one which can be conducted equally well, perhaps, within the format of the novel and the treatise.

My own view is that philosophy is not a genre of discourse, but simply a genealogical linkage connecting certain past figures with certain present figures—not a thread running through the rope, in Wittgenstein's figure, but just a way of noting that there is an ancestral relation of overlapping fibers. That was my point when I said that philosophy is delimited not by form or maker but by tradition. However, in the passage from *Consequences of Pragmatism* to which you refer, I did refer to philosophy as a "literary genre." That was a mistake, for the word "genre" suggests format, and I did not mean to do that.

So my answer to your question "Will you grant that the very concept of philosophy is a generic concept?" must, I think be "No." In the sense in which I think you intend the term "generic concept," I take it, whether something is instance of that concept can be established without reference to historical or cultural context. This may be true of pictorial art or of music, in the sense that these are distinct from written words in obvious, intercultural and transhistorical ways. But when it comes to distinguishing among written words, I do not think that we have a way of dividing up texts which meets your requirements.

To get an interesting classification of written texts, one needs to answer the question: what other texts are relevant to this one? Answering this question often does help one block out the written word into areas. Chemical treatises cluster together, for example, as do love stories. But the most interesting texts, usually, are the ones which Geertz describes as blurring genre-divisions. Most of the truly original and history-changing texts are of this sort—they are texts which were, on their first appearance, rather unlike anything that had previously been seen. (Think of Plato's *Dialogues*, for example, or of Machiavelli's *The Prince*, or Hegel's *Phenomenology of Spirit*.) The really important texts are the ones that render our old classifications unsatisfactory and force us to think up new ones.

I am quite willing to agree that Husserl was, as I am, too ignorant of Indian texts to know whether they are classifiable with the help of terms like "epistemology," "metaphysics," or "logic." But I should confess that I would be disappointed if all of them *were* so classifiable. My worry about the effort you suggest be made "by professional philosophers to acquaint themselves with the intellectual traditions to which they have been hitherto closed" is that professional philosophers are likely to import such classifications whether they are of any use or not. It is not that I wish to deny that it would do professional philosophers, or professionals of any other sort, good to increase their range of reading. It is rather that I distrust the process by which they decide what to read.

My hunch is that our sense of where to connect up Indian and Western texts will change dramatically when and if people who have read quite a few of both begin to write books which are not clearly identifiable as belonging to any particular genre, and are not clearly identifiable as either Western or Eastern. Consider, as an example, the novels of Salman Rushdie. There is no good answer to the question of whether he is an English or a Pakistani novelist, nor to whether *Shame* is a contribution to political journalism or to mythology, or *The Satanic Verses* a contribution to Islamic thought or to the novel of manners. Rushdie seems to me the sort of figure who has read a lot of books coming from the two sides of the world, and is likely to help create a culture within which intellectuals from both sides may meet and communicate.

I do not have any idea what a Rushdie whose tastes ran more to philosophy would be like, nor, indeed, whether there may not have already been such a person. But I am pretty sure that until such people come along—people who can bounce back and forth, with verve and irony, between the two sets of texts—that we are not going to make much progress in figuring out which books are best suited to be brought together. I agree that we do not need what you call "sophisticated *a priori* arguments designed to inquire where there is philosophy and where it is non-existent." But I think that the only "devices which will make us familiar with each other's traditions" are surprising, blurry, hard-to-classify books. These books will be written not as aids to intercultural understanding, but for special private purposes, by writers who have special private needs.

Let me turn once again to the question of whether there is an argument which would show that the virtues typical of the democratic West are commendable for the entire world? I can't imagine that any argument could ever show anything of the sort, any more than any argument could show that the West should devote itself to the study of Khomeini, or of Paramahansa Yogananda, or of Confucius. To have such an argument would be to have premises which were neutral between traditions and cultures. I cannot imagine such premises being found. The only premises common to all cultures are too banal to be of use—they are exemplified by the laws of logic, prohibitions against incest or against commercial fraud, and (to give an example to which I shall recur below) an insistence on the subordination of women to men.

I quite agree with you that consensus cannot be achieved if "the 'other' has not been present in the meeting." But to get a meeting going between people from two traditions more than presence is required. A lot of imagination is required also. My hunch is that the best vehicle for such imaginative flights will be texts which are neither comparisons and contrasts between previously-delimited domains within traditions, nor comparisons between traditions as a whole, but works of brilliant bricolage—

books which insouciantly bring together bits and pieces of each tradition in ways which do not fit under any previously formulated generic concept.

I agree that one person's mild ethnocentrism is another's secondary narcissism or cultural imperialism. But I see no way to avoid ethnocentrism except the blurring of ethnic—the sort of blurring represented by works of bricolage. I am in no position to write such works, so all I can do is cheer from the sidelines when somebody seems to have done so. I cannot offer what you call for: a "direct response" to charges of cultural imperialism. For such a response would be what my opponents would see as a confession of guilt: an admission that I am, like almost everyone else, working by my own parochial lights.

These lights suggest to me that the vocabulary of the "twentieth-century Western social democratic intellectuals" may well be the best anybody has yet come up with. I assuredly have no argument for this claim, and have no idea in what vocabulary such an argument could be phrased. But I think that the intellectuals I have in mind have had more experience than most other people at trying to enlarge their imaginations, trying to avoid parochialism, trying to see all sides—more experience, in short, of tolerance. I may be quite wrong about this. But, until another batch of people more experienced and skilled at tolerance comes to my attention, I probably shall not change my mind.

This unavoidable parochialism is going to infect any answer I could give to your request for more information about what my "vision really is regarding the 'future cosmopolitan society'." All I can offer are familiar Western clichés: e.g., that such a society would not be riven by tribal or religious or sectional warfare. It would not be so riven, because larger units (large nations which encompass many different races and religions, such as India and the U.S., or the human species itself) would have become objects of loyalty in the way in which tribes or races or religions had previously been objects of loyalty.

I regard such larger units as semi-deliberate, entirely artificial, creations. People like Jefferson and Gandhi devoted much of their lives to trying to create such units. Sometimes they succeeded and sometimes they failed; in some cases, we do not yet know whether they succeeded or failed. Philosophers have often tried to claim that the human species is itself a "natural" unit, an object of loyalty as well as a biological classification. I doubt that philosophy is well suited to make an object of loyalty out of the species, but I can vaguely imagine that someday the combined efforts of politicians, journalists, and novelists might make a single global community out of us.

One reason why I think that philosophers may not be of much use in creating such larger objects of loyalty is the one you give when you say "it is just not enough to say 'The pragmatist drops the revolutionary rhetoric of emancipation and unmasking . . . in favor of a reformist rhetoric of increased tolerance and decreased suffering'." Certainly it is not enough. This level of abstraction—talk about comparative rhetorics—is not what the situation demands. But that just shows, it seems to me, that philosophy professors are not the best people for the job. It doesn't show that pragmatism is not much of a philosophy, but only that pragmatism—like other philosophical schools—is itself a rather parochial movement.

You go on to ask whether traditional, non-pragmatic, appeals to principle will not be more effective if they are received as derived from something other than "the practices of the members of a given society." This question seems to me to reflect Plato's hope that there is something called "human reason" which transcends acculturation, and appeals to premises which everybody would acknowledge. To indicate why I distrust this Platonic idea as much as I do, let me turn to the topic of feminism.

Allan Bloom has suggested that Plato's description of his ideal state in *The Republic*—a description which specifies that women and men are to be given equal roles in governance cannot have been seriously meant. He takes the inclusion of this proposal for sexual equality as an indication that the entire scenario is meant ironically. He is doubtless right that Plato's audience would have been inclined to wonder whether Plato could seriously have imagined women sharing in the rule of states. But more important, the same wonder would have occurred to any ordinary person in almost any culture prior to relatively recent decades. One of the best examples of a truly intercultural universal seems

71

to be the subordination of women; this seems to be one conviction which emanates, if any conviction does, from what philosophers like to call "human reason," rather than from any particular historical tradition or cultural background.

Nevertheless, my notion of an egalitarian and cosmopolitan utopia includes the realization of the feminists' dreams. In such a utopia, gender would be as irrelevant to status and self-image as race. So when I ask myself what philosophers might do to help bring about such a utopia, I often ask myself whether there is anything in particular they could do for feminism.

It is not clear to me that there is. More particularly, it is not clear to me that the rhetoric of universal human rights, which you prefer to that of pragmatism, is of any use here. This rhetoric has been in the air for two hundred years or so, and very few of its exponents have thought that "humans" in the relevant sense included females. Contemporary feminists seem to me right in saying that "person" in the Western philosophical tradition has meant "male person." (Before women were given the right to be elected to the federal legislature in Canada, the relevant clause in the constitution read "all persons." When feminists pointed out that women were persons, the courts were able to say that they had never been taken to be such, in the relevant sense, so presumably they were not). In this situation, it seems to me that both pragmatist and non-pragmatist philosophers would have been stymied for arguments. They could appeal neither to the intentions of the framers of the document nor to consensus of the electorate, nor to the history of humanity.

What might help, it seems to me, is being able to point to particular subcultures in which women were treated as well as men. There are not many examples to point to, but there have been more and more in the course of the twentieth century. If one asks why these subcultures should be imitated, one is in the same position as when asked why non-Western cultures should take their lead from Western ones. No non-question-begging answer seems available—no neutral ground on which to debate the issue. If one asks how these subcultures have come into existence, I think the only answer is: by chance, by hook and crook, by certain groups being influenced by all sorts of odd considerations. Nevertheless, if one asks what sort of intellectuals have done most to bring such subcultures into existence, I think the answer would be the journalists and the novelists, rather than the theorists.

To suggest, as you do, that we need meta-narratives, and universalistic philosophical theories, as a platform to condemn, e.g., patriarchy, suggests that such metanarratives or such theories have some intrinsic appeal—some appeal apart from those aspects of some community's practice which they abstract from and generalize. I cannot see what such an intrinsic appeal might consist in. That is why I am a pragmatist—why I think that moral and political progress is a matter of playing one part of a community's practice off against other parts, rather than of comparing the practice as a whole with an ideal which is currently reflected by no practices. The slow and partial progress which women have made toward being thought of as persons by males has, it seems to me, been achieved by playing off internal tensions within patriarchal practice against one another, rather than by opening the eyes of the patriarchy to truths unreflected in practice. So I think that as long as we philosophers persist in thinking that our skill is in detecting universals, rather than simply in winking at tensions, we shall be less useful than we might otherwise be.

This is also why I think that the task of a philosophical theoretician at the present time may, in fact, consist largely in what you call "denouncing the essentialistic story of human affairs"—in denouncing, in Deweyan tones, the idea that there are moral universals out there to be appealed to, as opposed to social innovations to be recommended. At least such denunciation would help feminists say "We grant that 99.99% of all the human communities that have ever existed have refused to consider women as full-fledged persons. But look at the few which have, and consider whether you do not wish to imitate them. Forget about what is essentially human, and recognize that humanity is what it will make of itself, and that it just might choose to include the other 50% of the species, the 50% who have been ignored so far."

To sum up, I agree that ethnocentrism is a ladder which we eventually hope to throw away. But, unless one is a full-fledged Platonist essentialist, there is no other ladder available to use. So, as a good pragmatist, I think that we should use it—should play off our preferred ethnic against others, rather than comparing them all with something that is not a set of actual, or at least concretely imagined, human practices.

With all good wishes,
Dick R.

Letter 5

Dear Dick,

Thank you very much for your letter, which I received while I was in Shimla, India. I was delighted to read your analysis of the contemporary situation pertaining to the question "why the theme of otherness has drawn so much attention from the academicians today." You agree with me about the vital contribution that is made by the technological civilization in setting up the academic stage—by bringing people together in a manner that was unthinkable by our ancestors. This in turn is provoking an intellectual challenge, which is currently expressed as the theme of cultural otherness. The subject, however, is a sensitive and a complex one. We are becoming aware of the many intricate issues pertaining to the dialogue of cultures. The discussions of these issues seem still to be at an early stage. The awareness, however, has dawned that a monologue, however erudite, will not do. It is evident that we need to create an intellectual space precisely to give us, what you describe as, "a sense of the really hard choices" that we have before us today. This need is reflected in your remark that in the Hawaii conference you felt that neither the Eastern nor the Western intellectuals quite got to see what are the "really hard choices" that are confronting their colleagues.

You have indicated that "an important feature of Western high culture" is "the love of the exotic," which since the time of the Romantics has played a decisive role in promoting the zest for "otherness." You also maintain that this love of the exotic is to be appreciated more as an "attempt to enlarge one's imagination" than that of "getting an authentic understanding of an old tradition or a new artistic movement." I will certainly agree with you that self-enlargement is one of the most important outcomes of our encounter with the other, yet I would like to insist on the need which, it seems to me, you are somewhat underemphasizing, that of an authentic understanding based on information. By this, however, I do not wish to imply that the outsider has merely "to get something right which is out there," or that the insiders of a given community have a set of unchanging thoughts or notions that simply can be handed over. However, every culture has a story of its own. An honest and genuine effort to acquaint ourselves with the central and the sub-plots of the story of those whom we seek to comprehend seems indispensable to me. This is especially so if it is an encounter with an old tradition, as it is likely to contain critiques within critiques. The story is perhaps relatively less complex when we confront a new movement, since its genesis can be traced back perhaps with greater ease, and its language is likely to be not so different from our own. How can one comprehend the concerns that the insiders' ongoing conversation reflects, unless we know how an influential text—an instrument of socialization, has been interpreted and reinterpreted, how a theme has been developed, to use your words, without "piling up information"? How can one hope to find, as you seem to do, "something in that tradition . . . which one can use for purposes of self-enlargement"?

In the case of a highly articulate culture like that of India or the West, I do not quite see that it is possible to enlarge our imagination without making this sort of an effort. In the context of such exchanges one is provoked to ask whether our educational institutions could not be more effective in providing us with more information. The West is in this matter sometimes rather parochial, it tends to ignore the discourses of other cultures (think of the philosophy departments). This is an area where, it seems, there is acute need for more critical thinking on the part of those who are involved in the actual policymaking that affects the programs of educational institutions. In your paper "Education, Socialization, and Individuation" (1989) you have strongly supported the idea of "piling up information" and have expressed, as your reply to your critics show, that you do not think that one "can encourage imagination without a preparation in memorized information, or encourage individual talent without imparting a shared tradition." It seems to me that this holds true also of such situations when one wishes to educate oneself about others. Moreover, a superficial attraction for the exotic (often misconstrued as love) may be even "a dangerous thing" (just like "a little learning"). There are many devastating examples of how such love of the exotic, without any attempt at an "authentic understanding," have lead to disasters. The sort of creative appropriation that you have in mind rarely happens without labor. Although I agree with you that a successful encounter enables one "to speak differently, to use different terms in characterizing oneself," I would like to emphasize that it leads one to do so also about the other. It is a game in which the players learn to question the stereotypes and clichés that vitiate our descriptions—not only about the self but about the other as well.

Imaginary difference, it seems to me, has often been the breeding ground of hostility whereas a real informed encounter with the other is enriching—an experience which lays bare before us alternative perspectives to things. By authentic understanding, I simply meant this sort of an involvement which discloses to us what "really the hard choices" are and that I believe is not to be taken as a task which can be left to the faculty of imagination alone. It is a game (and as is the rule in all games, the players need to be prepared even when they know that the outcome is unpredictable) in which there are unexpected moments when perceptions of new horizons impress upon one in such a manner that one cannot but leave behind the customary practices of speaking about "otherness" and feel "forced to speak differently." Perhaps there is no impasse between knowledge and imagination, between finding and making— could it be that it is only in the interest of theory-making that we are inclined to say so? The contending theories of truth block our way, constrain our language, persuade us to deny at all cost the illuminating insights contained in a rival theory.

Cosmopolitanism is perhaps an awareness which lets thrive the ethnic differences for the benefit of an interdependent global community, an awareness that such a society is not what we can hope to *find* but which we together have to *make* and that it is an enterprise which requires a genuine effort to know each other—a process which requires, as you have said, "a lot of imagination."

Sometimes I wonder whether something important could be achieved if philosophers join forces with the politicians the novelists and the journalists, whom you consider (rightly, I think), to be effective agents for trying "to make an object of loyalty out of the species." You have expressed your doubts about the usefulness of the role of philosophers in this game. I, however, am inclined to believe that they can make a valuable contribution to this endeavor in bringing about a change, in persuading us to abandon, for example, the customary habits of speaking about gender, race, nationalities—about all who have been marginalized, who have never occupied the central space in the dominant discourse. If this could be achieved through the combined efforts of all concerned, the consequences will be radical. The "global interdependent society"—a phrase which the twentieth-century philosophers incessantly use—is a state of affair of utterly unequal opportunities. Whatever may be the way to social progress, one of the initial tasks lies in radically changing the modes of descriptions, especially while depicting the "otherness" of those whom we today, at last, publicly acknowledge as "oppressed," such as women everywhere, the blacks in U.S. or the large masses of humankind who inhabit those parts of the globe which is euphemistically called "the third world." To declare the ineffectivity of philosophers may be thought to be, and some have openly said so, a complicity with the status quo. Perhaps the involvement and active support of the pragmatists will be of help in making manifest the social constraints which dampen the political fervor that is needed to put egalitarian ideas into action, in pointing out which descriptions of the self and the other are no more useful for the day to day business of humankind. I felt encouraged to read that philosophical problems are "disguised forms of practical problems" and that your slogan is "if it doesn't make a difference to our practices, it makes no difference at all." If the pragmatists know that "we face a range of choices," it is incumbent upon them to show what these choices are in the context of a dialogue of cultures as well. This is precisely why I cannot accept that philosophers are not important agents in our plural world.

Philosophical doctrines have been seen, not for nothing, as vestiges of "discourses of power"— Nietzsche was seen as the philosopher of German Nazism, Dewey was perceived as the philosopher of American imperialism and the pragmatists are sometimes seen, for example by the American cultural left, as socially irresponsible. Regardless of whether these readings are correct or not, the point to note is that philosophers matter; their ideas are of consequence. The more of them will dare to cross the boundaries, the better for the intellectual life of the future generation. The least I hope is that we will hear a new set of questions from those who have encountered others and have not merely tried to leave it to their imagination what they are like. Perhaps our conversations about such notions as "common good," "better world," and "global village" would make more sense when we will know adequately what others' narratives are, when we will pile up some more information about how others live, how they go about doing what is called "thinking."

I am indeed very pleased to know what you thought was missing in the Hawaii conference as that gives me the clue to not only what you were seeking but also what you think needs to be achieved, *viz.*, how do "philosophers from the West and those from the East" gradually find "common options to discuss, options . . . what William James called 'live, immediate and forced'."

Evidently, I do not dream of seeing such a task being accomplished in one or several conferences, yet looking forward to our next conference to be held in India, I rejoice thinking that it is at least a step forward in this direction. Any imaginative effort to make the academicians conscious (especially because they are involved in activities that are designed to influence the young minds) of the demand of social engagement, of the need to take into consideration the intellectual life of the interdependent global community is to be welcomed. This seems to be sometimes conspicuously absent as recent discussions on various issues related to the general theme of cultural otherness have made us aware. It is amazing to take note of the lack of balance in the intellectual exchange in the scholarly life of the global community. Perhaps the following comment of Alisdaire McIntyre is of interest in this connection (from his review of *Beyond Marxism* by Vrajendra Raj Mehta [New Delhi, 1978], in *Political Theory* 2/4 [November 1983]: 623):

> The Indian political theorist has a harder task than his Western counterpart. He first of all has to be a good deal more learned, for he is required to know the history of Western political thought as well as the history of Asian thought. . . . He has to possess an array of linguistic skills that are uncharacteristic nowadays of Western political theories.
>
> Second, he has to sustain a relationship with his Western colleagues in which he takes their concerns with a seriousness that they rarely, unless they are among the very few Western specialists in Indian politics, reciprocate. Thus, a genuine dialogue is for the most part lacking. It is we in the West who are impoverished by our failure to sustain our part in this dialogue.

It will be interesting to hear your comments.

The philosophical stage always had and will have different kinds of people; a perusal of history of ideas, whether in India or in the West bears witness to that. To deny difference is a move which is decidedly antiphilosophy. There are fascinating records of competing paradigms for understanding the human situation even in pre-Buddhist India. The scene in the West is equally complex. I suppose that there are bound to be different readings about what the philosophical enterprise really is about. The essentialists, the pragmatists as well as those who are seen as both antiessentialist and antipragmatist (cf. M. Okrent's *Heidegger's Pragmatism* [Cornell University Press, 1988]) are all philosophers who will have different stories to tell about the complex relation between knowledge and power. I come to this question perhaps a little abruptly, and that is because, I think, this is not by any means unrelated to the question what role philosophers can play in "making an object of loyalty out of the species." I will appreciate if you would please elaborate what you see entailed in the idea that "knowledge is power" and what is gained when this is replaced by "power is all that there is to knowledge." This query is also not unrelated to the demand that a sustained critique of the role of the university and by implication of the role of knowledge in society is essential. In what ways are universities institutions of emancipation or domination of human beings?

I agree with you that there are not quite that many adequate books which can lend valuable insights into relevant issues of intercultural dimension. You have observed that such books, which "are not clearly identifiable as either Western or Eastern" are specially suited to stimulate and promote such awareness and have also indicated that only those who have read "a lot of books coming from the two sides of the world" are "likely to help create a culture within which intellectuals from both sides may meet and communicate." I am very pleased with this description, but I wish you would analyze further an example of such a book and illuminate us about the configuration of emotional, intellectual components that make the work appear that way. The fact that it is difficult to see whether a work is "Western" or "Eastern," I wonder how you accommodate that in your ethnocentric frame, and what it implies for what has happened to the sense of ethnic identity of the author. If you grant that boundaries can be crossed, how far are we—in theory—from some form of universalism?

Is there any hope that such works will be written oftener if our educational systems made works of other traditions more easily accessible to us instead of leaving the matter entirely to the personal idiosyncracy and private need of an individual determined to leave the beaten track? After all, if books of a certain kind are created all the time and others, desirable as they may be, are admittedly rare, there is a story which is pressing for attention. I cannot guess it but I have a hunch that somehow it is because our educational institutions, very largely, are preoccupied with "national narratives" and projecting a story of "otherness" which is not fostering the sense of "global interdependent society" in any honest sense. To say this is not to imply what ultimate purpose educational institutions should serve—I agree with you wholeheartedly that it is not possible to give a criterion of growth even when we acknowledge that growth is the ideal of education, and that "Hope—the ability to believe that the future will be unspecifiably different from, and unspecifiably freer than, the past—is the condition of growth." However, I cannot quite see how socialization, which is admittedly one of the goals of our education, stop at the threshold of just one nation or a tradition and occasionally pay lip-service to the so-called "global community." The theme of "cultural otherness" needs to be given more attention, if the next generation is to be "socialized in a somewhat different way" than we ourselves were socialized.

Speaking about growth brings me to another important aspect of this complex and difficult question. You seem to be enthusiastic about the Western model of growth and think that it has created "a culture of social hope." You dream of a future "egalitarian society—one in which basic needs are so well satisfied that individual differences of talent and opportunity do not arouse the sort of jealousy and resentment which made previous history a struggle between haves and have-nots."

In your letter to me, you have indicated that for you "the hope for the future" lies in the "Europeanization" of the globe. I wish to understand the idea clearly: What is in it that "Marx hoped for and Heidegger dreaded"? What is it that you see in this that although you cannot "justify this scenario by appeal to philosophical principles or to any other claim to knowledge" yet you feel that you "have no better scenario to write"?

Many in the "third world" look forward to social change yet do not wish it to be in the direction of Westernization. Despite their profound admiration for much of what the West has achieved, they sense the built-in pitfalls of the system. They see colonialism (which can be also of various kinds), war and exploitation of the oppressed groups—all as parts of it. Think of Gandhi, or Aurobindo—who in many ways are otherwise different kind of people—who saw the inevitable and the inescapable crisis in the Western model of growth. Is this distrust unfounded?

Although I do not think that his metaphors of "sick and deceived" are the most effective ones to portray the relation between the so-called developed and the developing nations, yet I think that serious attention should be paid when some observers, like Roger Garaudy (in his foreword to Ashis Nandy's book cited below), claim that much of the poverty of the third world is "created by the growth of the West . . . [that] the growth of some countries and the underdevelopment of others are the two faces of the same planetary maldevelopment. . . .[that] there cannot be a new world economic order without a new world cultural order." There are many critics of this Western model of growth, and of its implications for the interrelationship between power and prosperity. This, however, does not mean that there is an ideal model elsewhere. Even if we admit that the global socio-economic situation is an exceedingly complex affair, nevertheless it is evident that a philosophy of culture cannot be commended which supports such a "successful" system of production whose failures are charted at length both by keenly observant outsiders and insiders. There is a need for a conversation between philosophers and those who deal with the intricacies of political economy. I am well aware how difficult the task is, yet a search for alternatives must proceed and in that agenda the non-Western utopias cannot be simply ignored.

Some scholars are as a matter of fact striving to express an alternative perspective to the dominant visions of the future and even to work out an alternative narrative of past history. I am thinking of the group of intellectuals who contribute to the *Subaltern Studies* (edited by Ranajit Guha and Gavatri Spivak Chakravorty [Delhi & New York: Oxford University Press, 1982–1989]).

I am also reminded of, in this connection, works which are sort of combined political-psychological analysis of various forms of man-made suffering, such as attempted by Ashis Nandy. In his book entitled *Traditions, Tyranny, and Utopias* (New York: Oxford University Press, 1987), while evaluating "utopias," he writes:

> No dialogue is possible with a utopia claiming a monopoly on compassion and social realism, or presuming itself to be holding the final key to social ethics and experience. Such a vision not merely devalues all heretics and outsiders as morally and cognitively inferior, it defines them as throwbacks to an earlier stage of culture and history, fit to be judged exclusively by the norms of the vision. . . . Implicitly some visions see other visions not merely as competing ideologics but as conspiracies against human reason and values. A dialogue with such hegemonic, parochial visions may become an invitation to ethnic suicide. The proselytizing visions especially, even when they are secular, have a tendency to devour other utopias, paradoxically by rejecting the otherness of the latter and by 'accepting' them as earlier stages of the evolution of the self.

In brief, the intellectual struggle to redefine, redescribe human relationships in this narrative of progress and power-sharing must continue. I would like to believe that the voice of the intellectuals who have dared to cross the boundaries, whose concern for the well-being of the interdependent global community is authentic (a word, the simple meaning of which is, as indicated in the *Oxford Dictionary*, not false, not counterfeit) will be heard. But that is precisely what is missing—we are missing a genuinely involved conversation among intellectuals of the East and the West about an important area of beliefs and concerns that touch upon the wide range of possibilities of our lives, which again is an interplay of choice and circumstance. We are not actively participating but are blindly following a path which is unable to cope with political complacency about issues that matter to us all but which are simply marginalized in the name of something or other. Feminism is also such a theme.

Please allow me to make a digression. I cannot recall any more which French newspaper it was that in the late 1960s used to advertise its own political analysis to its potential readers by saying: *Si vous ne le suivez consciemment, vous le suivez aveuglement.* As I used to see this ad almost every evening on my way back home from the Sorbonne, I often wondered which is the largest groups of people who are in a sense politically blind-folded in a manner so that they will follow a course, laid out by nature and culture, with the least resistance? I do not need to tell you the answer that flashed in my mind. Two decades have passed since then. While I regret that gender is still a relevant factor in every step of our struggle for survival, I acknowledge that something has been achieved regarding the situation of women, the most important event being that the silence is broken. There is, as it is evident, still a long and difficult way in front of us— from thought to speech to action, from the private to the public realm of our existence.

I appreciate your concern when you say that you often ask yourself "whether there is anything in particular that [philosophers] might do for feminism?" However, it seems to me that you are not asking it as adamantly as is needed. This perhaps holds true of most of them who are otherwise concerned. It is just not enough to come up with, as you do, "It is not clear to me that there is"—this is not an acceptable answer.

We have to be able to say that we cannot "take no for an answer," like Gandhi did facing the mighty oppressors. In fact, I wish that we could imitate him and acquire the ability to put the oppressor to shame, even in his own eyes, to make the oppressed aware of her strength and proceed with the Himalayan stubbornness to achieve what we have set ourselves to do. The opposition to a state of affair where "gender will be . . . irrelevant to status and self-image" is perhaps more formidable than what Gandhi was facing. In his struggle, however, he recognized at least some vital aspects of the feminist aspiration. I recall in this connection his message sent to the All India Women's Conference in 1936 where he said that "When woman, whom we call *abala*, becomes *sabala*, all those who are helpless will become powerful" (*bala* means strength, the prefixes *a* and *sa* carry respectively the senses "without" and "with").

It seems to me that despite all the harm that the dominant male discourse has done to the image and self-image of women, I do not think that anything will be gained by turning the issue into a battle between the sexes. I think that the war that needs to be waged is against a system, a system in which if women are the victims, men also pay a heavy price; a system that was impossible to fight in those days when technological civilization did not open up the possibilities of colossal changes that are present today: improved transportation, communication, and most important— in a woman's life—improved means for intervening in nature's design for reproduction.

Nothing much will be gained simply by replacing the rhetoric of "human rights" by that of pragmatism—it seems to me that you are getting too fond of labels. If idioms of modern theories of interpretation are all that were necessary (I am not saying that it is of no help—as a matter of fact I am sensitive to the misleading use of certain idioms and metaphors, specifically when they are loaded with implications of which we are not fully aware. May I remind you, in this connection that I am very curious to hear your comments on how the Kantian metaphor has influenced Western culture theorists—a remark that you made in a letter to me in the context of discussion about cyclic and linear time) to bring about the desired state of affair (a goal about which we are in perfect agreement) why do you sound so pessimistic even at the thought of bringing about the feminist utopia? The point is to detect why the society is not moving faster to implement the changes that are needed and about which there is today a general consensus (is there?). It is immaterial to me whether it is a reiteration of human rights or that of the pragmatic idioms that will persuade the society to perceive a woman as a person—if any of these separately or combined or even some new innovations can make a headway in doing the job—I will say "Bravo." If you are disillusioned with the idioms of human rights in getting the society to see the woman as fully "human," show us how the pragmatist can be truly effective in bringing about his egalitarian dream come true, at least in the academic world where he is heard. How can a "good pragmatist"—as you say you are—allow himself to remain ineffective in the face of the most important task of our time and simply give up by saying that "it does not seem" that there is much that philosophers can do to help bring about the feminist utopia! I hope that you will be able to get your pen to flow (they say that the pen is mightier than the sword), reminding all those who specially need to be reminded that you do not "take no for an answer."

There are narratives of domination and exploitation in every society, whether in the past or now, whether in the East or in the West. This web of human relationships gives rise to institutions, which in turn legitimizes, sanctions such practices that are current in a given society. The job of the insider critics is precisely to point out where the system is failing and what possibilities the future holds for us. The East is no exception to that. "Hopes of a freer and more equal future generation" is perhaps not only Western, as you seem to think. Obviously we need to spell out more clearly what are the shared visions, the shared commitments of the East and the West today. The network of exchanges will surely decide how the question of global unity will be treated, how we will handle the threat and the hope created by the technological civilization. The shrewder we will become in the management of conflicts, the more we will learn how to use nonviolent tactics in all forms of negotiations, whether we will acknowledge persuasion rather than force in the name of an eternal order or god or on simple pragmatic grounds matters little. I admit that each one of these options has the power of persuasion—not every idiom works on everyone, even when what each one is striving to achieve is not pronouncedly different from the other.

At the end of your second letter to me, you write that "Ethnocentrism is a ladder which we eventually hope to throw away." If we can hope to do away with it, is ethnocentrism then a description of a provisional state of human inter-relationship or is it an idiom one clings to for want of a more adequate one? May I request you again to elaborate on your view of "mild ethnocentrism"—an idea which some have interpreted as a form of cultural imperialism (obviously a highly exaggerated remark which is evident from what you write at the end of your second letter; but your answer to this serious objection in your previous letter was too brief).

The relationship between East and West has had several phases—we have heard of the dichotomies, we have heard of the need of a synthesis. Some have wondered whether a "fusion of horizons" will take place, some claim it to be an accomplished fact. In any case the need for a fresh self-understanding and a review of alterity are still awaiting subtler and more powerful formulations. The success of technological civilization has increased the urge and the possibility for meeting of minds across boundaries than ever before. The Indian soil, where the next meeting of Philosophy East-West is scheduled to take place under the auspices of the Indian Council of Philosophical Research, is traditionally considered fertile for questioning the assumption that "never the twain shall meet." Welcome to India.

With best wishes,

Sincerely,
Anindita N. Balslev

Letter 6

Dear Anindita,

Thanks for your letter of October 14. You raise a great many issues, and I shall try to take up under separate headings.

I. *East-West Asymmetry*: I quite agree with MacIntyre, in the passage you quote, that Eastern writers and thinkers have done much more work than Western ones to find out what goes on the other side of the world. I also agree with him that "It is we in the West who are impoverished by our failure to sustain our part in this dialogue." So I agree with those who urge that we in the West should try to make higher (and perhaps secondary) education more multicultural. I agree that imagination without information is empty, and that we in the West have not exerted ourselves enough to get relevant information.

On the other hand, there are practical questions for the West which need to be thought about, and which I haven't seen any good answers to. Suppose you are designing a multicultural curriculum for Western students (ages 18–20, say) a curriculum in which the Plato-the Christian Scriptures-Shakespeare-Newton-Goethe-Marx-Darwin canon is to be supplemented in such a way as to make a global community more attainable. The two principal questions you face, I think, are: How do you get the additions to the canon to seem more than pointless hurdles to be leaped? How much territory do you try to take in?

On the first question: I take it that lots of students in India and Africa around 1900 were made to pass examinations on *Hamlet* and Plato's *Republic* without any clear sense of why they were

89

reading these books, what they were supposed to do with them, or why they were supposed to be important. All they knew was that if they didn't pass the exams, they wouldn't get good positions. If you simply stick some Upanishads and some Analects into contemporary Western curricula, the same problem will arise. These texts will be seen in the way in which the Analects were seen by most candidates for the Chinese imperial civil service, or Greek prosody by most candidates for the nineteenth-century British Foreign Service. The only way in which these texts might come to mean something to the students would be if they were taught by people who have some sense of the social institutions within which these texts were composed, of the traditions of interpretation to which they have given rise, and the uses to which they have been put—the sort of sense which some British teachers in India and Africa had in regard to Shakespeare and Plato.

The only way around this impasse for the foreseeable future, as far as I can see, is for the West to import large numbers of people from other cultures to teach the texts of those cultures by filling in the backgrounds of those texts. I should certainly like to see this happen, but I can foresee a lot of problems. One is brain drain; one doesn't want the best minds of the non-West going off to spend their lives teaching in other countries. It is not clear that the non-West has, as yet, *enough* intellectuals to engage in a large-scale *mission civilizatrice*. Another, and perhaps greater, problem is the one I posed above: Which cultures, and how many cultures?

This is more of a problem for the West than it has been for the East, because the Christian-scientific-technological West of the nineteenth century—the great period of imperialism and thus of indoctrination of non-Westerners with Western ideas—was comparatively homogeneous and monolithic when compared with the diversity of alternatives to it. When the contemporary West looks outside itself, it sees an Islamic tradition, two great Indian traditions (Hinduism and Buddhism), a Chinese tradition, and a Japanese tradition, each of which has at least as much coherence, and requires as much study to grasp, as does the West. (This is to ignore entirely, for the sake of simplicity, native African traditions or native American traditions.) I find it hard to imagine that any single person is going to assimilate the information necessary to grasp imaginatively how the West has managed to patch up a synthesis between the Epistles of Paul and the Darwinian account of the descent of man, why Islam thinks the Koran so beautiful, why Hindus think the caste system something more than an outdated moral abomination, how a Buddhist who is also a social democrat can reconcile the struggle for social reform with a belief in the desirability of attaining Nirvana, why the Chinese still find it profitable to go on and on about Confucius, and why the Japanese find Western individualism so peculiarly repellent. These are all things I should like to understand myself. But I despair of doing so—not just because I am now almost sixty, but because I have never met anybody who even claimed to understand all six of these things. So I suspect that the best we can hope for, in a multicultural curriculum for the West, is to tell students to learn something about one, or at the most two, non-Western cultures, while blithely ignoring the others. This awkward result seems to me obscured by loose talk, fairly common in the West these days, about "non-Western ideas"—as if there were one great big source of ideas called the non-West.

How did this asymmetry come to be? That is, how did the West come to be a more or less compulsory subject for people in the East, but not vice versa? The simple, and largely correct, answer is: Because the West was where the money and the power were coming from. This suggests that until the money and the power begin to flow the other way we are going to have a hard time persuading Western youth to look beyond the West—a situation which may be partially remedied by Japan becoming the primary source of preferment for ambitious young Americans, and the Arab world becoming the primary source for ambitious young Europeans.

But there is a further, more complicated, answer to the question about the source of the present asymmetry. This is that the West itself provides most of the promising tools for undoing what the West has been doing to the non-West. If you were, during the first sixty years of this century, an Arab or an African or an Indian impatient to get out from under the colonialist yoke, what you used were (except in the case of Gandhi and his movement)

Western guns, Western political and socio-economic categories, Western ideas for social reform, Western means of communication (printing presses or telephones) and so on. This was because the devices and categories inherited from your previous traditions just weren't of much use in anti-colonialist struggles. (Whether the case of Gandhi forms the exception that disproves the rule, I just don't know. I doubt it, but here I have to confess a lot of ignorance.)

My hunch is that more Western science and technology is about the only thing that can cope with the results of prior Western science and technology. For example: only condoms and pills (made ever cheaper by technological ingenuity) can cope with the effects of Western medicine on the death rate in various places; only Western bureaucratic rationality can cope with the famines caused by the colonialists' elimination of earlier agricultural methods; only institutions of the sort Foucault condemned as "panoptic" can prevent the exploitation of the peasants by the landowners. If this hunch is right, then the asymmetry which MacIntyre notes is bound to persist, unless and until some non-Western nation or community can make a go of a general abjuration of Western science and technology.

This brings me to the point you make about Gandhi, Aurobindo, and others having "seen the inevitable and inescapable crisis in the Western model of growth." I'm inclined to ask: What's so Western about it? All big powerful empires—East and West—have gone in for economic growth and political expansion, and most have eventually fallen of their own weight when they ran out of steam. If one views the former colonial powers as still constituting an economic empire, then it is quite likely, I agree, that this empire too will fall—if not because it runs out of sources of energy and raw materials, then because of environmental catastrophe, or because of bloody revolution caused by the immiseration of the oppressed (in the form, say, of an Iraqi or Argentine nuclear attack on Europe and America). But that just brings us back to the question: are there cultural resources in the non-West that can help stave off the catastrophes westernization is likely to bring about? Maybe there are, but I don't know where, and I haven't seen any very helpful suggestions about where we might locate them. Maybe it is true that, as Susan Sontag, once said, "The white race is the cancer of the planet." But the analogy suggests that to fend off, defeat or reverse the spread of this cancer, something different is needed from the traditional ways of living which the non-cancerous cells were pursuing before being attacked.

This makes me suspicious of Roger Garaudy's claim (which you quote) that "There cannot be a new world economic order without a new world cultural order." I could see the point if it were reversed: if one said that a new cultural order presupposed a new economic order—one in which all the money and power weren't concentrated in the Northern Hemisphere, for example. But I have no idea what sort of new 'cultural order' would be the basis for a redistribution of money and power. The West's best guess about what such an order might be is something like "a universal and sincere acceptance of the ideals common to the French Revolution and the early Christians." I doubt that this is the sort of thing Garaudy has in mind. But unless the non-West can lay sketch of a different new cultural order, I doubt that the West will give up its belief that only the as-yet-unrealized ideals of the West stand between the global community and its destruction at the hands of the West. As with technology, so with Western ideals—they themselves may be the best medicine for the ills they cause. Or they may not be. But it is not a reason for doubting their efficacy that they came from the same part of the world as the evils they hope to defeat.

II. *The Efficacy of Philosophy*: Let me now switch topics to the issue about which, I suspect, our disagreement is most intractable. When I say that it is not clear to me that there is much that philosophy can do for feminism, you say that this "is not an acceptable answer." It is as if we had utterly different pictures of what sort of thing philosophy is. I regard it as one of the more peripheral of the academic disciplines—one which once had a considerable importance, but has been declining in efficacy and status in recent centuries thanks to the rise of other disciplines. You, I gather, regard it as the repository of an awesome moral responsibility. I am not sure how to get out of this impasse.

You say at one point that "philosophical doctrines have been seen, not for nothing, as vestiges of 'discourses of power'." That seems to me merely to say that philosophers, like religious prophets, scientists, novelists, and everybody else, have often been made use of by people who had power and wanted more power. Sure, what else would one expect? I would be bothered by this only if I thought there was some kind of discourse that was *not* a "discourse of power." I see all discourse as ways of communicating beliefs and desires, and all human beliefs (artistic as much as scientific beliefs, philosophical as much as theological beliefs, Buddhist as much as Nietzschean beliefs) as tools for fulfilling human desires. What I mean by saying "power is all there is to knowledge" (a question you raise elsewhere) is just that knowledge is justified true belief, and that the true belief is the one (among the available alternatives) which gets you what you want. In the neutral and vegetarian sense in which I am using "power," everybody always wants power and always will, for power is just the ability to gratify your desires (for food, sex, Nirvana, domination, humility, or whatever).

From the fact that all knowledge is an instrument of power it does not follow that, as you claim, "philosophers matter; their ideas are of consequence." Nor does this follow from the fact that Mussolini used Nietzsche, Jefferson used Locke, Stalin used Marx, or Roosevelt used Dewey. Sure, philosophers have often mattered, but then so have astrologers and shamans. The question is how much they matter—of what consequence their ideas are—for the issue at hand: how to establish a global community.

You say that "to declare the ineffectivity of philosophers may be thought to be, and some have openly said so, a complicity with the status quo." That charge would be sensible if it were the case that status quos only got changed by philosophers coming up with some effective ideas. But nobody really believes that, do they? Why might there not be a bad status quo which philosophy could not help with but which some other discipline could (e.g., medicine, economics, engineering, architecture)? What is so special about philosophy, why is it that when an engineer or a mathematician says "sorry, but at the moment I have nothing on hand useful for your purposes" he or she is not betraying civilization, but when a philosopher says it he or she is?

There is of course a broad, etymological sense of "philosophy" in which it means "the love, or pursuit, of wisdom." Used in that broad sense, I suppose, to say that philosophy can't help is to say that thought, reflection, deliberation, can't help. That would, indeed, be a bad thing to say. But who uses "philosophy" in this sense these days? Who thinks that you and I, people who specialized in the study of philosophy in our youth, are more engaged in, or more likely to succeed in, the pursuit of wisdom than our contemporaries who specialized in medicine, law, politics, or the arts? Who thinks that we philosophy professors are better at thinking, deliberating, and reflecting than the rest of the educated public?

You say that "If the pragmatists know that 'we face a range of choices,' it is incumbent upon them to show what these choices are in the context of a dialogue of cultures as well." Why? It isn't just pragmatists who know we face a range of choices. Everybody knows that. Everybody hopes that cultures other than their own will help with choices which seem beyond the resources of their own culture. But why think that pragmatist philosophers have some special responsibility here? *Qua* pragmatists, they are merely making the negative point that we needn't bother with Platonic and Cartesian questions about foundations for knowledge, or Kantian questions about unconditional moral obligations, or various other bad questions (that is, questions the answers to which didn't make any difference to practice) which are familiar from the philosophical tradition. This rubbish-removing, or ground-clearing, job is all that pragmatism is, as far as I can see, good for. It gets some of the debris of the Western philosophical tradition out of the way. Perhaps, for all I know, it might be useful in getting some of the debris of some non-Western traditions out of the way. But when it is asked to do something for the organization of a global community other than this rubbish-removing task, I doubt that it has much to offer.

III. *Feminism and Philosophy*: Perhaps this is the point to move on to something you say later in your letter: "It is immaterial to me whether it is a reiteration of human rights or that of the pragmatic idioms that will persuade the society to perceive a woman as a person. If any of these separately or combined or even some new innovations can make headway in doing the job, I shall say 'Bravo'." Me too. But that's just the sort of reason I have for not expecting as much of philosophy professors as you seem to. Lots of different sorts of philosophy professors, holding wildly different philosophical views, can and do unite in support of feminism. Which philosophical view is going to be most useful to the feminist cause depends upon what rhetoric is most effective in raising feminist consciousness, and what rhetoric is most effective in getting the patriarchs to see a bit of the light.

In the U.S., there are large numbers of philosophers who identify themselves as "feminist philosophers"; feminist philosophy is now a recognized sub-area of philosophical inquiry. But the feminist philosophers disagree widely among themselves about almost all the traditional philosophical issues. They do not possess a tool, or a weapon, called "philosophy" to put at the service of feminism—for there is no unitary thing to bear this name. They just put whatever dialectical skill they may have in the service of working out defenses (sometimes on the basis of theories of natural right, sometimes on the basis of Derridean theories of language, using whatever ammunition comes to hand) of feminist political measures. So it seems to me pointless to ask that pragmatist philosophy professors be, in your phrase, "truly effective in making the egalitarian dream come true." That's like asking that the people who repair the treads on the tanks be "truly effective in winning the war"; such people do their bit, but a bit is all they can do. Philosophy is not a magic wand which can make dreams come true, and a set of philosophical doctrines (such as pragmatism) is not to be judged on the basis of its efficacy in doing so. To make this sort of demand on a philosophical view is to treat the philosophers of different schools as if they were the priests of different religions, priests each of whom claimed special access to a divine Being whose wrath and power they could call down on the enemy army, and whose claims to serve the One True God are to be judged on the basis of our own army's success.

As it happens, I have recently been writing about what pragmatism might do for feminism. All I came up with was the possibility that one line of thought associated with pragmatism, Deweyan historicism, might be of some use in providing feminists with a little extra rhetorical ammunition. Dewey's historicism might, I think, be useful in helping us see the point of the feminists' frequent anger and frustration over the "common sense" quality of patriarchal customs. By synthesizing Hegel and Darwin, Dewey helped give us a sense of how moral progress is made not by appealing to "eternal truths" but by the rise of new ways of speaking—new vocabularies which permit things to sound plausible which previously sounded so *un*-common-sensical as to be simply whacky. So when feminists like Catherine MacKinnon and Marilyn Frye speak of "a new voice" and a "struggle with meaninglessness," of the need to extend logical space beyond what the language of a patriarchal society has envisaged, a Deweyan historicist can offer a useful metatheory which brings out the analogy between the rise of feminism, the rise of Christianity, the rise of Galilean science, the Romantic Movement, and the like. Supplying such a meta-theory—showing how feminism fits into an Hegelian, if not into a Kantian, account of moral progress—is not much, but it may be all pragmatism can do in this area.

Still, there is one other suggestion which, I think, pragmatists might usefully make to feminists: that they drop the quasi-Kantian notion of "women's experience" or "women's perspective" or "women's standpoint." There has been much criticism recently, in the literature of feminist philosophy in the U.S., of "feminist essentialism"—of attempts to specify what is distinctively female, what the distinctive "otherness" of the feminine is. As a pragmatist, I am sympathetic to this criticism, as I am to all forms of anti-essentialism. I am also sympathetic to what Sellars calls "psychological nominalism"—the doctrine that all awareness is a *linguistic* affair. On this view, there is no such thing as "inarticulate experience" which is then expressed in language. For such philosophers of language as Davidson and Sellars, language is not a medium of expression for something prior called "experience." So, *a fortiori*, there is no pre-linguistic state called "feminine experience" which needs to be articulated in language.

From this perspective, the task of feminist intellectuals is not to express what women have timelessly, ahistorically, been—to spell out their previously unknown inner essence but to find ways of describing their public situation, their constant oppression, which makes it easier and easier for women to see that oppression as evitable, as not part of the nature of things. The point is not to make audible or visible what has been hidden—to bring reality to light and displace mere appearance, or to make inarticulate experience articulate—but rather to bring something into existence which has not previously existed. What is to be created is a strong, autonomous, vociferous, sort of woman, one who will pay no attention whatever to the traditional gender-distinctions built into the language and customs of her time. Such a woman might or might not find some use for philosophy, but philosophers might make some minor contribution to her emergence by replacing the traditional from-appearance-by-reality philosophical model of social progress with a pragmatist, evolutionary, model. [See my "Feminism and Pragmatism," *Michigan Quarterly Review* (Spring 1991), for more on these matters.]

IV. *Otherness*: This brings me back to the topic with which I began my first letter to you: otherness. I find this topic a bit baffling. This is because, as a good pragmatist, I am uncomfortable with notions of uncommunicability, with the idea that some special sorts of things (God, the inside of another human being, the experience of the oppressed) are impossible, or at least very difficult, to put into language. When I am told that the oppressed are very different from me, a white male inhabitant of the richest part of the globe, I am inclined to say "Of course they are. They have a lot less money and power, they are always on the edge of starvation and always threatened by brutality, and I'm not. That makes them very different all right, but it doesn't raise any deep philosophical question about our relations, or our knowledge of each other. It just raises practical questions of how to redistribute money and power—how to get a global socio-economic system going that will level things off."

I think there will seem to be a *philosophically* interesting difference between the experience of the oppressed and mine only if one adopts a Kantian notion of "conditions of experience" and thinks that the weak and the strong, or the women and the men, or the West and the East, have something like different Kantian "forms of intuition" or "categories of understanding"—so different that people whose experiences are conditioned by one set of structures cannot have any sense of what it is like to have experiences conditioned by another set. (This is the sort of suggestion which you have taken up, in regard to Western and Indian conceptions of time, in your own work). Such Kantian metaphors of structure and content (and the consequent talk about the space, or the time, or the cosmos of different cultures being incommensurably different) seems to me not only optional, but, in its effects, mischievous. Its only function is to inspire scepticism, or a kind of sentimental longing for the unknowable. If we are psychological nominalists, dispensing with "experience" in favor of language, and if we follow Davidson in saying that there is no such thing as an unlearnable language, then we can say that all that "otherness" comes down to is the fact that practices (including linguistic practices) suitable for dealing with one (human and social) environment are often ill-adapted for other environments. So the interesting difference between sets of practices is not that between those developed for dealing with environment A (e.g., the backwoods of Nagaland, the slums of Calcutta, the interior of the Sahel) and environment B (e.g., the middle-class suburbs of the Northern Hemisphere), but between those that presently exist and those that are just a gleam in somebody's eye.

As examples of those which are still just a gleam in somebody's eye, consider those suggested by Christ or the Buddha to the first generations of their disciples, or, once again, those gradually being developed by contemporary feminists. These are practices which are not yet in place, practices which, if they some day become widespread, might help change the environment in which people live. Many contemporary leftist intellectuals suggest that in order to end the oppression of women and of the weak and the poor we must develop such new practices. (They often suggest also—though, for reasons given above, I cannot see why— that it is the special responsibility of philosophy professors to invent such new practices). But there seems to me an enormous difference between the contemporary situation of women and the contemporary situation of the weak and poor.

Women have been conditioned throughout the centuries to believe that they are naturally subordinate, that God or Nature has unfortunately made them incapable of autonomy, of taking part in political deliberation, of wisdom, etc. Large numbers of women in our times *still*, alas, believe something like this. The weak and the poor have often, in the past (as in the Hindu or Japanese caste systems, or in Calvinist doctrines of salvation), been conditioned to believe that they are somehow singled out by nature for misery. But I do not think that now in most parts of the world, they any longer believe anything of the sort. Thanks to the secularizing influences of the recent West, it has become increasingly difficult to use religion to sanctify oppression. (This seems to me one almost *entirely* good thing which Westernization has done for the East, though I admit that the Western colonialists tried to use Christianity to legitimize their own oppression when they first arrived.) It has become increasingly easier for the weak and the poor to see themselves as victims of the greed of their fellow-humans rather than of Destiny, or the gods, or of the sins of their ancestors.

So, though I think that women still are in the process of working out a new set of practices, the weak and the poor are *already* enmeshed in a practice of calculating who gets what out of their labor and suffering. Their problem is not how to conceive of themselves, how to create themselves (as it still is for women) but simply of how to wrest control of a greater share of wealth and power without making things still worse in the process—how to create a social revolution which is not a worse remedy than the disease it was fomented to cure.

I hope that you will not tell me that it is my duty, as a pragmatist, or as a philosopher, to come up with a solution to this problem. Whether it's my duty or not, I in fact have nothing to offer. Though I was brought up to be a socialist, I no longer want to nationalize the means of production (because the experience of Central and Eastern Europe suggests that nationalization is, to put it mildly, no help in redistributing wealth and power). I suspect we are stuck with market economies—which means with private property for the foreseeable future. I should love to suggest ways of reconciling market economies with social justice, but all I can come up with is the standard European-model welfare state—a solution which seems to have no clear relevance to the choices presently before the electorates of, e.g., India or Brazil. I hope that in the next century new alternatives appear—ones of the sort suggested by, for example, Roberto Unger in his *Politics*, ones which try to work out alternatives to both socialism and capitalism. But I do not think that my pragmatism, or my philosophical expertise, are of any particular use to the construction of such alternatives.

To sum up: I am not sure that either what you call "the theme of cultural otherness," or philosophy, has much relevance to the question of how to get wealth and power more evenly redistributed. For purposes of such redistribution, the differences between cultural traditions may just not matter very much. Economic and bureaucratic rationality—the sort which, as far as I can see, we are going to have to use to solve problems of redistribution—will, I hope, just slide over cultural divisions, leaving as many of them in place as possible. My ideal world is one in which there is enough equality in wealth and power so that people are more or less free to continue or change cultural traditions as it suits them. The only alternative that I can see is the kind of isolation which, e.g., China and Japan imposed upon themselves until the nineteenth century— but that isolation was a result of the rich and powerful within the society using cultural otherness as a device for perpetuating their own oppressive rule.

There is a tendency in contemporary political discussion to treat "the West" as a name for the source of every imaginable oppression—to lump bureaucratic rationality, patriarchy, colonialism, capitalism, technology, and every other oppressive institution one can think of together and call the result "the West." This lumping serves no good purpose. The West did not invent oppression, and it is, like every other culture, a polychrome tangle of institutions and traditions—some of which may be useful only to the oppressors, some only to the oppressed, but most to both. If there is any general lesson which pragmatism preaches, it is to deessentialize, to break up the lump, to pick over these traditions and institutions one by one, and see what use they have for our present purposes.

With all good wishes,
Dick R.

Appendix

Philosophers, Novelists, and Intercultural Comparisons: Heidegger, Kundera, and Dickens

Richard Rorty

Suppose that the nations which make up what we call "the West" vanish tomorrow, wiped out by thermonuclear bombs. Suppose that only Eastern Asia and sub-Saharan Africa remain inhabitable, and that in these regions the reaction to the catastrophe is a ruthless campaign of de-Westernization—a fairly successful attempt to obliterate the memory of the last three hundred years. But imagine also that, in the midst of this de-Westernizing campaign, a few people, mostly in the universities, squirrel away as many souvenirs of the West—books, magazines, small artifacts, reproductions of works of art, movie films, videotapes, and so on—as they can conceal.

Now imagine that, around the year 2500, memory of the catastrophe fades, the sealed-off cellars are uncovered, and artists and scholars begin to tell stories about the West. There will be many different stories, with many different morals. One such story might center on increasing technological mastery, another on the development of artistic forms, another on changes in sociopolitical institutions, and another on the lifting of sexual taboos. There would be dozens of other guiding threads which storytellers might seize upon. The relative interest and usefulness of each will depend upon the particular needs of the various African and Asian societies within which they are disseminated.

If, however, there are *philosophers* among the people who write such stories, we can imagine controversies arising about what was "paradigmatically" Western, about the *essence* of the West. We can imagine attempts to tie all these stories together, and to reduce them to one—the one true account of the West, pointing out the one true moral of its career. We think of *philosophers* as prone to make such attempts because we tend to identify an area of a culture as "philosophy" when we note an attempt to substitute theory for narrative, a tendency toward essentialism. Essentialism has been fruitful in many areas—most notably in helping us to see elegant mathematical relationships behind complex motions, and perspicuous microstructures behind confusing macro-structures. But we have gradually become suspicious of essentialism as applied to human affairs, in areas such as history, sociology, and anthropology. The attempt to find laws of history or essences of cultures—to substitute theory for narrative as an aid to understanding ourselves, others, and the options which we present to one another—has been notoriously unfruitful. Writings as diverse as Karl Popper's on Hegel and Marx, Charles Taylor's on positivistic social science, and Alasdair MacIntyre's or Michael Oakeshott's on the importance of traditions have helped us realize this unfruitfulness.

Despite growing recognition that the essentialistic habits of thought which pay off in the natural sciences do not assist moral and political reflection, we Western philosophers still show a distressing tendency to essentialism when we offer intercultural comparisons. This comes out most clearly in our recent willingness to talk about "the West" not as an ongoing, suspenseful adventure in which we are participating but rather as a structure which we can step back from, inspect at a distance. This willingness is partly the cause, and partly the effect, of the profound influence of Nietzsche and Heidegger on contemporary Western intellectual life. It reflects the sociopolitical pessimism which has afflicted European and American intellectuals ever since we gave up on socialism without becoming any fonder of capitalism—ever since Marx ceased to present an alternative to Nietzsche and

Heidegger. This pessimism, which often calls itself "postmodernism," is a rueful sense that the hopes for greater freedom and equality which mark the recent history of the West were somehow deeply self-deceptive. Postmodernist attempts to encapsulate and sum up the West have made it increasingly tempting to contrast the West as a whole with the rest of the world as a whole. Such attempts make it easy to start using "the East" or "non-Western modes of thought" as the names of a mysterious redemptive force, as something which may still offer hope.

In this essay, I shall be protesting against this recent tendency to encapsulate the West, to treat it as a finished-off object which we are now in a position to subject to structural analysis. In particular, I want to protest against the tendency to take Heidegger's account of the West for granted. There is, it seems to me, a growing willingness to read Heidegger as the West's final message to the world. This message consists largely of the claim that the West has, to use one of Heidegger's favorite phrases, "exhausted its possibilities." Heidegger was one of the great synoptic imaginations of our century, but his extraordinary gifts make his message sound more plausible than I think it is. We need to remember that the scope of Heidegger's imagination, great as it was, was largely restricted to philosophy and lyric poetry, to the writings of those to whom he awarded the title of "Thinker" or of "Poet." Heidegger thought that the essence of a historical epoch could be discovered by reading the works of the characteristic philosopher of that epoch and identifying his "Understanding of Being." He thought that the history of the West could best be understood by finding a dialectical progression connecting the works of successive great philosophical thinkers. Philosophers by trade are especially susceptible to the persuasive power of Heidegger's account of the West's history and prospects. But I think that this susceptibility is a professional deformation which we should struggle to overcome.

As a way of counteracting Heidegger and, more generally, the kind of post-Heideggerian thinking which refuses to see the West as a continuing adventure, I want to put forward Dickens as a sort of anti-Heidegger. I can sum up my sense of the respective importance of Dickens and Heidegger by saying that, if my imaginary

Asians and Africans were, for some reason, unable to preserve the works of both men, I should much prefer that they preserve Dickens'. For Dickens could help them grasp a complex of attitudes that was important to the West, and perhaps unique to the West, in a way that neither Heidegger nor any other philosopher could. The example of Dickens could help them think of the novel, and particularly the novel of moral protest, rather than of the philosophical treatise, as the genre in which the West excelled. Focusing on this genre would help them to see not technology, but rather the hope of freedom and equality as the West's most important legacy. From the point of view I shall be adopting, the interaction of West and East is better exemplified by the playing of Beethoven's Ninth Symphony in Tienanmen Square than by the steel mills of Korea or the influence of Japanese prints on Van Gogh.[1]

To lay out this point of view, I shall do three things in the remainder of this essay. First, I shall offer an account of Heidegger as one more example of what Nietzsche called "the ascetic priest." Second, I shall summarize and gloss Milan Kundera's account of the novel as the vehicle of a revolt against the ontotheological treatise, of an anticlerical reaction against the cultural dominance of the ascetic priests. Third, I shall use Dickens to illustrate Kundera's suggestion that the novel is the characteristic genre of democracy, the genre most closely associated with the struggle for freedom and equality.

Heidegger's later work was an attempt to provide the one right answer to the question asked by my imaginary African and Asian philosophers of the future. Heidegger would advise these philosophers to start thinking about the West by thinking about what killed it—technology— and to work backward from there. With a bit of luck, they could then recreate the story which Heidegger himself told, the story he called "the history of Being." For Heidegger, the West begins with the pre-Socratics, with what he calls the separation between the "what" and the "that." This separation between what a thing is in itself and the relations which it has to other things engenders distinctions between essence and accident, reality and appearance, objective and subjective, rational and irrational, scientific and unscientific, and the like—all the dualisms which mark off epochs in the history of an increasing lust for power, an increased inability to let beings be. This is the history which Heidegger summarizes in Nietzsche's phrase *die Wüste wächst*, the wasteland spreads.[2]

As Heidegger tells this story, it culminates in what he calls the "age of the world-picture," the age in which everything is Enframed, seen as providing an occasion either for manipulation or for aesthetic delectation. It is an age of giantism, of aesthetico-technological frenzy. It is the age in which people build 100-megaton bombs, slash down rain forests, try to create art more thoroughly postmodern than last year's, and bring hundreds of philosophers together to compare their respective world pictures. Heidegger sees all these activities as aspects of a single phenomenon: the age of the world picture is the age in which human beings become entirely forgetful of Being, entirely oblivious to the possibility that anything can stand outside a means-end relationship.

Seeing matters in this way is an instance of what Habermas describes as Heidegger's characteristic "abstraction by essentialization." In 1935 Heidegger saw Stalin's Russia and Roosevelt's America as "metaphysically speaking, the same." In 1945 he saw the Holocaust and the expulsion of ethnic Germans from Eastern Europe as two instances of the same phenomenon. As Habermas puts it, "under the leveling gaze of the philosopher of Being even the extermination of the Jews seems merely an event equivalent to many others."[3] Heidegger specializes in rising above the need to calculate relative quantities of human happiness, in taking a larger view. For him successful and unsuccessful adventures—Ghandi's success and Dubček's failure, for example—are just surface perturbations, distractions from essence by accidents, hindrances to an understanding of what is *really* going on.

Heidegger's refusal to take much interest in the Holocaust typifies the urge to look beneath or behind the narrative of the West for the *essence* of the West, the urge which separates the philosophers from the novelists. Someone dominated by this urge will tell a story only as part of the process of clearing away appearance in order to reveal reality. Narrative is, for Heidegger, always a second-rate genre—a tempting but dangerous one. At the beginning of *Sein und Zeit*, Heidegger warned against the temptation to confuse ontology with the attempt to tell a story that relates beings to other beings, *mython tina diegeisthai.*[4] At the end of his career he takes back his earlier suggestion that what he called "the task of thinking" might be accomplished by *Seinsgeschichte,* by telling a story about how metaphysics and the West exhausted their possibilities. Now he realizes that he must cease to tell stories about metaphysics, must leave metaphysics to itself, if he is ever to undertake this task.[5]

Despite this suspicion of epic and preference for lyric, the ability to spin a dramatic tale was Heidegger's greatest gift. What is most memorable and original in his writings, it seems to me, the new dialectical pattern he finds in the sequence of canonical Western philosophical texts. His clue to this pattern was, I think, Nietzsche's construal of the ascetic priests' attempts at wisdom, contemplation, and imperturbability as furtive and resentful expressions of those priests' will to power.

Heidegger, however, tried to out-Nietzsche Nietzsche by reading Nietzsche himself as the last of the metaphysicians. He hoped thereby to free himself from the resentment which, despite himself, Nietzsche displayed so conspicuously. Heidegger thought that if he could free himself from this resentment, and from the urge to dominate, he could free himself from the West and so, as he said, quoting Hölderlin, "sing a new song." He thought that he could become free of the will to power as a result of having seen through its last disguise. He thought that by leaving metaphysics to itself, turning from *Seinsgeschichte* to *Denken,* from *Sein* to *Ereignis,* he could accomplish the transition from epic to lyric, turn from the West to something Wholly Other than the West.

But on my reading, Heidegger was simply one more ascetic priest and his attempt to encapsulate the West, to sum it up and distance himself from it, was one more power play. Heidegger was intensely aware of the danger that he was making such a play. But to be intensely aware of the danger is not necessarily to escape it. On my reading, Heidegger is still doing the same sort of thing that Plato tried to do when he created a supersensible world from which to look down on Athens, or Augustine when he imagined a City of God from which to look down on the Dark Ages. He is opting out of the struggles of his fellow humans by making his mind its own place, his own story the only story that counts, making himself the redeemer of his time precisely by his abstention from action. All that Heidegger manages to do is to historicize the Platonic divided line. He tips it over on its side. The Heideggerian counterpart of Plato's world of appearance seen from above is the West seen from beyond metaphysics. Whereas Plato looks down, Heidegger looks back. But both are hoping to distance themselves from, cleanse themselves of, what they are looking at.

This hope leads both men to the thought that there must be some purificatory askesis which can render them fit for intercourse with something Wholly Other—for impregnation by the Form of the Good, for example, or for Openness to Being. This thought is obviously an important part of the Western tradition, and it has obvious analogues (and perhaps sources) in the East. That is why Heidegger is the twentieth-century Western thinker most frequently "put into dialogue" with Eastern philosophy.[6] Such Heideggerian themes as the need to put aside the relations between beings and beings, to escape from busy-ness, to become receptive to the splendor of the simple, are easy to find in the East.

But there are other elements in Western thought, the elements which Heidegger despised, which are much harder to put into dialogue with anything in the East. In particular, as I shall be saying in more detail shortly, there is the novel—a Rabelaisian response to the ascetic priests. So, insofar as we philosophers become content either with a dialogue between Plato and the East or with one between Heidegger and the East, we may be taking the easy way out of the problems of intercultural comparison. Insofar as we concentrate on philosophy, we may find ourselves concentrating on a certain specific human type which can be counted upon to appear in *any* culture—the ascetic priest, the person who wants to set himself apart from his fellow humans by making contact with what he calls his "true self" or "Being" or "Brahman" or "Nothingness."

All of us philosophers have at least a bit of the ascetic priest in us. We all hanker after essence and share a taste for theory as opposed to narrative. If we did not, we should probably have gone into some other line of work. So we have to be careful not to let this taste seduce us into the presumption that, when it comes to other cultures, only our counterparts, those with tastes similar to our own, are reliable sources of information. We should stay alert to the possibility that comparative philosophy not only is not a royal road to intercultural comparison, but may even be a distraction from such comparison. For it may turn out that we are really comparing nothing more than the adaptations of a single transcultural character type to different environments.

Those who embody this character type are always trying to wash the language of their respective tribes off their tongues. The ascetic priest finds this language *vicious*, in Sartre's sense. His ambition is to get above, or past, or out of, what can be said in language. His goal is always the ineffable. Insofar as he is forced to use language, he wants a language which either gives a purer sense to the words of the tribe or, better yet, a language entirely disengaged from the business of the tribe, irrelevant to the mere pursuit of pleasure and avoidance of pain. Only such a person can share Nietzsche's and Heidegger's contempt for the people whom Nietzsche called "the last men." Only he can see the point of Heidegger's disdainful remark that the greatest disaster—the spread of the wasteland, *die Verwüstung der Erde*, understood as the forgetfulness of Being—may "easily go hand in hand with a guaranteed living standard for all men, and with a uniform state of happiness for all men."' Ascetic priests have no patience with people who think that mere happiness or mere decrease of suffering might compensate for *Seinvergessenheit*, for an inability to be in touch with something Wholly Other.

My description of the ascetic priest is deliberately pejorative and gendered. I am sketching a portrait of a phallocentric obsessive, someone whose attitude toward women typically resembles Socrates' attitude when he was asked whether there are Forms of hair and mud. Such a person shares Nietzsche's endlessly repeated desire for, above all else cleanliness. He also shares Heidegger's endlessly repeated desire for simplicity. He has the same attitude toward sexual as to economic commerce: he finds it messy. So he is inclined both to keep women in their traditional subordinate place, out of sight and out of mind, and to favor a caste system which ranks the manly warriors, who bathe frequently, above the smelly traders in the bazaar. But the warrior is, of course, outranked by the priest—who bathes even more frequently and is still manlier. The priest is manlier because what is important is not the fleshly phallus but the immaterial one—the one which penetrates through the veil of appearances and makes contact with true reality, reaches the light at the end of the tunnel in a way that the warrior never can.

It is easy, with the help of people like Rabelais, Nietzsche, Freud, and Derrida, to make such seekers after ineffability and immateriality sound obnoxious. But to do them justice, we should remind ourselves that ascetic priests are very useful people. It is unlikely that there would have been much high culture in either West or East if there had not been a lot of ascetic priests in each place. For the result of trying to find a language different from the tribe's is to enrich the language of later generations of the tribe. The more ascetic priests a society can afford to support, the more surplus value is available to provide these priests with the leisure to fantasize, the richer and more diverse the language and projects of that society are likely to become. The spin-offs from private projects of purification turn out to have enormous social utility. Ascetic priests are often not much fun to be around, and usually are useless if what you are interested in is happiness, but they have been the traditional vehicles of linguistic novelty, the means by which a culture is able to have a future interestingly different from its past. They have enabled cultures to change themselves, to break out of tradition into a previously unimagined future.

My purpose in this essay, however, is not to arrive at a final, just evaluation either of Heidegger in particular or of ascetic priests in general. Instead, it is to develop an antithesis between the ascetic taste for theory, simplicity, structure, abstraction, and essence and the novelist's taste for narrative, detail, diversity, and accident. From now on, I shall be preaching a sermon on the following text from Kundera's *The Art of the Novel:*

> The novel's wisdom is different from that of philosophy. The novel is born not of the theoretical spirit but of the spirit of humor. One of Europe's major failures is that it never understood the most European of the arts—the novel; neither its spirit, nor its great knowledge and discoveries, or the autonomy of its history. The art

inspired by God's laughter does not by nature serve ideological certitudes, it contradicts them. Like Penelope, it undoes each night the tapestry that the theologians, philosophers and learned men have woven the day before.

. . . I do not feel qualified to debate those who blame Voltaire for the gulag. But I do feel qualified to say: The eighteenth century is not only the century of Rousseau, of Voltaire, of Holbach; it is also (perhaps above all!) the age of Fielding, Sterne, Goethe, Laclos.[8]

The first moral I draw from this passage is that we should stay on the lookout, when we survey other cultures, for the rise of new genres—genres which arise in reaction to, and as an alternative to, the attempt to *theorize* about human affairs. We are likely to get more interesting, and more practically useful, East-West comparisons if we supplement dialogues between our respective theoretical traditions with dialogues between our respective traditions of antitheory. In particular, it would help us Western philosophers get our bearings in the East if we could identify some Eastern cultural traditions which made fun of Eastern philosophy. The kind of fun I have in mind is not the in-house kind which we philosophers make of one another (for example, the kind of fun which Plato makes of Protagoras, Hume of natural theology, Kierkegaard of Hegel, or Derrida of Heidegger). It is rather that made by people who either could not follow a philosophical argument if they tried, or by people who have no wish to try. We need to be on the lookout not just for Japanese Heideggers, Indian Platos, and Chinese Humes, but for Chinese Sternes and Indonesian Rabelaises. I am too ignorant to know whether there *are* any people of the latter sort, but I hope and trust that there are. Somewhere in the East there *must* have been people who enjoyed unweaving the tapestries which the saints and sages had woven.

The need to unweave these tapestries can be thought of as the revenge of the vulgar upon the priests' indifference to the greatest happiness of the greatest number. This indifference is illustrated by the way in which Horkheimer and Adorno look for a dialectic of Enlightenment which will permit them to weave *Candide* into the same pattern as Auschwitz, the way in which they allow contemplation of that pattern to convince them that Enlightenment hopes were vain. It is also illustrated by the way in which

Heidegger blurs the distinction between automobile factories and death camps. We philosophers not only want to see dialectical patterns invisible to the vulgar, we want these patterns to be clues to the outcomes of world-historical dramas. For all our ascetism, we want to see ourselves, and people like ourselves, as engaged in something more than merely private projects. We want to relate our private obsessions, our private fantasies of purity, novelty, and autonomy, to something larger than ourselves, something with causal power, something hidden and underlying which secretly determines the course of human affairs.[9]

From Kundera's point of view, the philosopher's essentialistic approach to human affairs, his attempt to substitute contemplation, dialectic, and destiny for adventure, narrative, and change, is a disingenuous way of saying: what matters for me takes precedence over what matters for you, entitles me to ignore what matters to you, because I am in touch with something—reality—with which you are not. The novelist's rejoinder to this is: it is comical to believe that one human being is more in touch with something nonhuman than another human being. It is comical to use one's quest for the ineffable Other as an excuse for ignoring other people's quite different quests. It is comical to think that *anyone* could transcend the quest for happiness, to think that any theory could be more than a means to happiness, that there is something called Truth which transcends pleasure and pain. The novelist sees us as Voltaire saw Leibniz, as Swift saw the scientists of Laputa, and as Orwell saw Marxist theoreticians—as comic figures. What is comic about us is that we make ourselves unable to see things which everybody else can see—things like decreased suffering and increased happiness—by convincing ourselves that these things are "mere appearance."

The novelist's substitute for the appearance–reality distinction is a display of diversity of points of view, a plurality of descriptions of the same events. What the novelist finds especially comic is the attempt to privilege one of these descriptions, to take it as an excuse for ignoring all the others. What he or she finds most heroic is not the ability sternly to reject all descriptions save one, but rather the ability to move back and forth between them. I take this to be the point Kundera is making when he says:

It is precisely in losing the certainty of truth and the unanimous agreement of others that man becomes an individual. The novel is the imaginary paradise of individuals. It is the territory where no one possesses the truth, neither Anna nor Karenin, but where everyone has the right to be understood, both Anna and Karenin.'°

Kundera is here making the term "the novel" roughly synonymous with "the democratic utopia"—with an imaginary future society in which nobody dreams of thinking that God, or the Truth, or the Nature of Things, is on her or his side. In such a utopia nobody would dream of thinking that there is something more real than pleasure or pain, or that there is a duty laid upon us which transcends the search for happiness. A democratic utopia would be a community in which tolerance and curiosity, rather than truth-seeking, are the chief intellectual virtues. It would be one in which there is nothing remotely approximating a state religion or a state philosophy. In such a community, all that is left of philosophy is the maxim of Mill's *On Liberty,* or of a Rabelaisian carnival: everybody can do what they want if they don't hurt anybody else while doing it. As Kundera says, "The world of one single Truth and the relative ambiguous world of the novel are molded of entirely different substances."

One can, if one likes, see Kundera and Heidegger as trying to overcome a common enemy: the tradition of Western metaphysics, the tradition which hints at the One True Description that exhibits the underlying pattern behind apparent diversity. But there is a big difference between what the two men propose as an alternative to this tradition. For Heidegger the opposite of metaphysics is Openness to Being, something most easily achieved in a pretechnological peasant community with unchanging customs. Heidegger's utopia is pastoral, a sparsely populated valley in the mountains, a valley in which life is given shape by its relationship to the primordial Fourfold—earth, sky, man, and gods. Kundera's utopia is carnivalesque, Dickensian, a crowd of eccentrics rejoicing in each other's idiosyncracies, curious for novelty rather nostalgic for primordiality. The bigger, more varied, and more boisterous the crowd the better. For Heidegger, the way to overcome the urge to domination is to take a step back and to see the West and its history of power plays from afar, as the sage sees the Wheel of Life from afar. For Kundera the way to overcome the urge to domination is to realize that everybody has and always will have this urge, but to insist that nobody is more or less justified in having it than anybody else. Nobody stands for the truth, or for Being, or for Thinking. Nobody stands for *anything* Other or Higher. We all just stand for ourselves, equal inhabitants of a paradise, of individuals in which everybody has the right to be understood but nobody has the right to rule.

Kundera summarizes his attitude toward the ascetic priest when he says:

> Man desires a world where good and evil can be clearly distinguished, for he has an innate and irrepressible desire to judge before he understands. Religions and ideologies are founded on this desire. . . . They require that somebody be right: either Anna Karenina is the victim of a narrow-minded tyrant, or Karenin is the victim of an immoral woman; either K. is an innocent man crushed by an unjust Court, or the Court represents divine justice and K. is guilty.
>
> This "either-or" encapsulates an inability to tolerate the essential relativity of things human, an inability to look squarely at the absence of the Supreme Judge.[11]

Kundera, in a brief allusion to Heidegger, politely interprets his term "forgetfulness of Being" as forgetfulness of this essential relativity.[12] But Heidegger never, even in his early "pragmatist" phase,[13] believed in essential relativity in Kundera's sense of the term. Heidegger's genre is the lyric, not the novel; his hero is Hölderlin, not Rabelais or Cervantes. For Heidegger the other human beings exist for the sake of the Thinker and the Poet. Where there is a Thinker or a Poet, there human life is justified, for there something Wholly Other touches and is touched. Where there is not, the wasteland spreads.

Whereas for Heidegger there are certain moments in certain lives which both redeem history and permit history to be encapsulated, for Kundera the thing to do with history is to keep it going, to throw oneself into it. But this throwing oneself into history is not the sort which is recommended by the ideological revolutionary. It is not a matter of replacing Tradition with Reason or Error with Truth. Kundera thinks that if we want to know what went wrong with the expectations of the Enlightenment we should read Flaubert rather than Horkheimer and Adorno. He says:

> Flaubert discovered stupidity. I daresay that is the greatest discovery of a century so proud of its scientific thought. Of course, even before Flaubert, people knew stupidity existed, but they understood it somewhat differently: it was considered a simple absence of knowledge, a defect correctable by education. Flaubert's vision of stupidity is this: Stupidity does not give way to science, technology, modernity, progress; on the contrary, it progresses right along with progress![14]

I take Kundera to be saying that the Enlightenment was wrong in hoping for an age without stupidity. The thing to hope for is, instead, an age in which the prevalent varieties of stupidity will cause less unnecessary pain than is caused in our age by our varieties of stupidity. To every age its own glory and its own stupidity. The job of the novelist is to keep us up to date on both. Because there is no Supreme Judge and no One Right Description, because there is no escape to a Wholly Other, this is the most important possible job. But it is a job which can only be undertaken with a whole heart by someone who is untroubled by dreams of an ahistorical framework within which human history is enacted, a universal human nature by reference to which history can be explained, or a far-off divine event toward which history moves. To appreciate the essential relativity of human affairs, in Kundera's sense, is to give up the last traces of the ascetic priest's attempt to escape from time and change, the last traces of the attempt to see us as actors in a drama already written before we came on the scene. Heidegger thought that he could escape from metaphysics, from the idea of a Single Truth, by historicizing Being and Truth. He thought that he could escape Platonic escapism by telling a story about the *Ereignis* which was the West, rather than about *Sein*. But from Kundera's point of view Heidegger's attempt was just one more attempt to escape from time and chance, though this time an escape into historicity rather than into eternity. For Kundera, eternity and historicity are equally comic, equally essentialist, notions.

The difference between Kundera's and Heidegger's reaction

to the Western metaphysical tradition comes out best in their attitude toward closure. It is as important for Kundera to see the Western adventure as open-ended—to envisage forever new sorts of novels, recording strange new joys and ingenious new stupidities—as it is for Heidegger to insist that the West has exhausted its possibilities. This comes out in Kundera's insistence that the novel does not have a *nature,* but *only* a history, that the novel is a "sequence of discoveries."[15] There is no Platonic Form for the novel as a genre to live up to, no essential structure which some novels exhibit better than others, any more than there exists such a Form or such a structure for human beings. The novel can no more exhaust its possibilities than human beings can exhaust their hope for happiness. As Kundera says, "The only context for grasping the novel's worth is the history of the European novel. The novelist need answer to no one but Cervantes."[16]

The same point emerges when Kundera insists that the history of the novel and of Europe cannot be judged by the actual political future of Europe—or by the actual fate, whatever it may be, of the West. In particular, the West blowing itself up with its own bombs should not be read as a judgment on the novel, or on Europe—nor should the coming of an endless totalitarian night. To do so would be like judging a human life by reference to some ludicrous accident which ends it violently, or like judging Western technology by reference to Auschwitz. As Kundera says:

> Once upon a time I too thought that the future was the only competent judge of our works and actions. Later on I understood that chasing after the future is the worst conformism of all, a craven flattery of the mighty. For the future is always mightier than the present. It will pass judgment upon us, of course. But without any competence.

Kundera continues:

> But if the future is not a value for me, then to what am I attached? To God? Country? The people? The individual? My answer is as ridiculous as it is sincere. I am attached to nothing but the depreci- ated legacy of Cervantes.[17]

Kundera's phrase "paradise of individuals" has an obvious application to Dickens, because the most celebrated and memorable feature of his novels is the unsubsumable, uncategorizable idiosyncracy of the characters. Dickens' characters resist being subsumed under moral typologies, being described as exhibiting these virtues and those vices. Instead, the names of Dickens' characters *take the place* of moral principles and of lists of virtues and vices. They do so by permitting us to describe each other as "a Skimpole," "a Mr. Pickwick," "a Gradgrind," "a Mrs. Jellaby," "a Florence Dombey." In a moral world based on what Kundera calls "the wisdom of the novel" moral comparisons and judgments would be made with the help of proper names rather than general terms or general principles. A society which took its moral vocabulary from novels rather than from ontico-theological or ontico-moral treatises would not ask itself questions about human nature, the point of human existence, or the meaning of human life. Rather, it would ask itself what we can do so as to get along with each other, how we can arrange things so as to be comfortable with one another, how institutions can be changed so that everyone's right to be understood has a better chance of being gratified.

To those who share Nietzsche's sense that the "last men" give off a bad smell, it will be ludicrous to suggest that *comfort* is the goal of human social organization and moral reflection. But this suggestion would not have seemed ludicrous to Dickens. That is why Dickens has been anathematized by Marxists and other ascetic priests as a "bourgeois reformer." The term "bourgeois" is the Marxist equivalent of Nietzsche's term "last man"—it stands for everything which the ascetic priest wants to wash off. For Marxism, like Platonism and Heideggerianism, wants more for human beings than comfort. It wants transformation, transformation according to a single universal plan; Marxists are continually envisaging what they call "new socialist man." Dickens did not want anybody to be transformed, except in one respect: he wanted everyone to notice and understand the people he or she passed on the street. He wanted people not to make each other uncomfortable by applying moral labels, but to recognize that all their fellow humans—Dombey and Mrs. Dombey, Anna and Karenin, K. and the Lord Chancellor—had a right to be understood.

Despite having no higher goal than comfortableness of human association, Dickens did an enormous amount for equality and freedom. The last line of Swift's self-written epitaph—"Imitate him if you dare: he served human liberty"[18]—would do for Dickens' tablet as well. But Dickens performed his services to human liberty not with the help of the "savage indignation" which Swift rightly ascribed to himself but with something more bourgeois— sentimental tears and what Orwell called "generous anger." Dickens strikes us as a more bourgeois writer than the man who described the Yahoos because he is more comfortable with, and hopeful for, human beings. One indication of this comfortableness is the fact on which Orwell remarked in the following passage:

> In *Oliver Twist, Hard Times, Bleak House, Little Dorrit,* Dickens attacked English institutions with a ferocity that has never since been approached. Yet he managed to do it without making himself hated, and, more than this, the very people he attacked have swallowed him so completely that he has become a national institution himself.[19]

The important point is that Dickens did not make himself hated. I take it that this was partly because he did not attack anything as abstract as "humanity as such," or the age or the society in which he lived, but rather concrete cases of particular people ignoring the suffering of other particular people. He was thus able to speak as "one of us"—as the voice of one who happened to notice something to which the rest of us could be counted upon to react with similar indignation as soon as we notice it.[20]

Dickens was, as Orwell says, "a good-tempered antinomian," a phrase which would apply equally to Rabelais, Montaigne, or Cervantes, but hardly to Luther or Voltaire or Marx. So I take "generous anger" to mean something like "anger which is without malignity because it assumes that the evil has merely to be noticed to be remedied." This was the kind of anger later found in Harriet Beecher Stowe and Martin Luther King, but not the kind of anger found in the ascetic priests. For the latter believe that social change is not a matter of mutual adjustment but of re-creation—that to make things better we must create a new kind of human being, one who is aware of reality rather than appearance. Their anger is *un*generous in the sense that it is aimed not at a lack of understanding of particular people by other particular people but rather at an ontological deficit common either to people in general or, at least, to all those of the present age. The generosity of Dickens', Stowe's, and King's anger comes out in their assumption that people merely need to turn their eyes toward those who are getting hurt and notice the *details* of the pain being suffered, rather than need to have their entire cognitive apparatus restructured.

As an empirical claim, this assumption is often falsified. As a moral attitude, it marks the difference between people who tell stories and people who construct theories about that which lies beyond our present imagination, because beyond our present language. I think that when Orwell identified a capacity for generous anger as the mark of "a free intelligence," he was adumbrating the same sort of opposition between the theorist and the novelist which I am trying to develop in this essay. Earlier I said that theorists like Heidegger saw narrative as always a second-best, a propaedeutic, to a grasp of something deeper than the visible detail, the true meaning behind the familiar and commonplace one. Novelists like Orwell and Dickens are inclined to see theory as always a second-best, never more than a reminder for a particular purpose, the purpose of telling a story better. I suggest that the history of social change in the modern West shows that the latter conception of the relation between narrative and theory is the more fruitful.

To say that it is more fruitful is just to say that, when you weigh the good and the bad that the social novelists have done against the good and the bad that the social theorists have done, you find yourself wishing that there had been more novels and fewer theories. You wish that the leaders of successful revolutions had read fewer books which gave them general ideas and more books which gave them an ability to identify imaginatively with those whom they were to rule. When you read books like Kolakowski's history of Marxism, you understand why the Party theoretician, the man responsible for the "correct ideological line," has always been, apart from the maximum leader himself, the most feared and hated member of the Central Committee. This may remind you that Guzman, the leader of the quasi-Maoist Sendero Luminoso movement in Peru, wrote his dissertation on Kant. It may also remind you that Heidegger's response to the imprisonment of his Social Democratic colleagues in 1933 came down to "Don't bother me with petty details."

The important thing about novelists as compared with theorists is that they are good at details. This is another reason why Dickens is a useful paradigm of the novel. To quote Orwell again, "The outstanding, unmistakable mark of Dickens' writing is the *unnecessary detail*"; "He is all fragments, all details—rotten architecture, but wonderful gargoyles—and never better than when he is building up some character who will later on be forced to act inconsistently."[21] If we make Dickens paradigmatic of the West, as I hope my fantasized Africans and Asians would, then we shall see what was most instructive about the recent history of the West in its increased ability to tolerate diversity. Viewed another way, this is an increased ability to treat apparent inconsistency not as something to be rejected as unreal or as evil, but as a mark of the inadequacy of our current vocabularies of explanation and adjudication.[22] This change in our treatment of apparent inconsistency is correlated with an increasing ability to be comfortable with a variety of different sorts of people, and therefore with an increasing ability to leave people alone to follow their own lights. This willingness is reflected in the rise of pluralistic bourgeois democracies, societies in which politics becomes a matter of sentimental calls for alleviation of suffering rather than of moral calls to greatness.

It may seem strange to attribute this sort of willingness to the recent West—a culture often said, with excellent reason, to be racist, sexist, and imperialist. But it is of course also a culture which is very *worried* about being racist, sexist, and imperialist, as well as about being Eurocentric, parochial, and intellectually intolerant. It is a culture which has become very conscious of its capacity for murderous intolerance and thereby perhaps more wary of intolerance, more sensitive to the desirability of diversity, than any other of which we have record. I have been suggesting that we Westerners owe this consciousness and this sensitivity more to our novelists than to our philosophers or to our poets.

When tolerance and comfortable togetherness become the watchwords of a society, one should no longer hope for world-historical greatness. If such greatness—radical difference from the past, a dazzlingly unimaginable future—is what one wants, ascetic priests like Plato, Heidegger, and Suslov will fill the bill. But if it is not, novelists like Cervantes, Dickens, and Kundera may suffice.[23] Because philosophy as a genre is closely associated with the quest for such greatness—with the attempt to focus all one's thoughts into a single narrow beam and send them out beyond the bounds of all that has been previously thought—it is among the *philosophers* of the West that contemporary Western self-hatred is most prevalent. It must be tempting for Africans and Asians— the principal victims of Western imperialism and racism—to see this self-hatred as about what the West deserves. But I would suggest that we take this self-hatred as just one more symptom of the old familiar quest for purity which runs through the annals of the ascetic priesthood in both East and West. If we set these annals to one side, we may have a better chance of finding something distinctive in the West which the East can use, and conversely.

Notes

1. The students were reported to have played a recording of this symphony as the troops were being held up by masses of people jamming the highways leading into the square. The same point about the impact of the West could be made by reference to the student speakers' repeated invocations of Thoreau and of Martin Luther King.

2. See Martin Heidegger, *What Is Called Thinking,* trans. by J. Glenn Gray (New York: Harper and Row, 1968), pp. 29 ff. (*Was Heisst Denken?* [Tübingen: Niemeyer, 1954], pp. 11 ff.).

3. J. Habermas, "Work and Weltanschauung: The Heidegger Controversy from a German Perspective," *Critical Inquiry* 15 (Winter 1989): p. 453.

4. Heidegger, *Sein und Zeit*, 10th ed. (Tübingen: Niemeyer, 1963), p 6.

5. See Heidegger, *On Time and Being,* trans. by Joan Stambaugh (New York: Harper and Row, 1972), pp. 24, 41 (*Zur Sache des Denkens* [Tübingen: Niemeyer, 1969], pp. 25, 44).

6. See, for example, Graham Parkes, ed., *Heidegger and Asian Thought* (Honolulu: University of Hawaii Press, 1987). As what I say below makes

clear, I have doubts about Parkes' claim (p. 2) that "Heidegger's claim to be the first Western thinker to have overcome the tradition should be taken more seriously if his thought can be brought to resonate deeply with ideas that arose in totally foreign cultural milieux, couched in more or less alien languages, over two millennia ago." This resonance can also be taken as a sign of regression rather than of transcendence—as a way of returning to the womb rather than a way of overcoming.

7. See Heidegger, *What Is Called Thinking?* p. 30 (*Was Heisst Denken?* p. 11). Heidegger goes on to say that Nietzsche's words *die Wüste wächst* "come from another realm than the appraisals of our age" (*ays einem anderen Ort als die gaengigen Beurteilungen unserer Zeit*). For another passage which brushes aside happiness as beneath the Thinker's consideration, see *The Question Concerning Technology*, trans. by W. Lovitt (New York: Harper and Row, 1977), p. 65 (*Holzwege* [Frankfurt: Klustermann, 1972], p. 204): "Metaphysics is history's open space wherein it becomes a destining that the suprasensory world, the Ideas, God, the moral law, the authority of reason, progress, the happiness of the greatest number, culture, civilization, suffer the loss of their constructive force and become void."

8. Kundera, *The Art of the Novel*, trans. by Linda Asher (New York: Grove Press, 1986), p. 160.

9. I discuss this urge, with reference to Heidegger, on pp. 107 f. and 119 f. of my *Contingency, Irony and Solidarity* (Cambridge: Cambridge University Press, 1989).

10. Kundera, *The Art of the Novel*, p. 159.

11. Ibid., p. 7

12. Ibid., p. 5. Here, at the beginning of his book, Kundera thinks of Husserl's *Lebenswelt* and Heidegger's *In-der-Welt-Sein* as standing over against "the one-sided nature of the European sciences, which reduced the world to a mere object of technical and mathematical investigation," and casually assimilates both to his own notion of "the essential relativity of human affairs." But this assimilation is overly polite, and misleading. Husserl and Heidegger were insistent on getting down to the basic, underlying structure of the *Lebenswelt*, or of *In-der-Welt-Sein*. For Kundera, we make up this structure as we go along.

13. See Mark Okrent, *Heidegger's Pragmatism* (Ithaca: Cornell University Press, 1988), for an account of Heidegger's career that distinguishes the pragmatism, the emphasis on *Vorwurf* and *Bezuglichkeit*, in *Sein und Zeit* from the post-*Kehre* quietism.

14. Ibid., p. 162.

15. Ibid., p. 14.

16. Ibid., p. 144.

17. Ibid., p. 20.

18. Yeats' translation of Swift's "... *imitare si poteris, strenuum pro virili libertatis vindicem.*"

19. George Orwell, *Collected Essays, Journalism and Letters,* vol. 1 (Harmondsworth: Penguin, 1968), pp. 414–415. In his illuminating *The Politics of Literary Reputation: The Making and Claiming of 'St. George' Orwell* (Oxford: Oxford University Press, 1989), John Rodden has noted both that Orwell in this essay "directly identified himself with Dickens" (p. 181) and that the identification worked, in the sense that "What Orwell wrote of Dickens [in the last sentence of the passage I have quoted] soon applied to himself" (p. 22). One facet of the identification was the patriotism common to the two men—a sense of identification with England and its history which trumped any theory about the place of England in universal history. From the theorist's point of view, patriotism is invariably suspicious, as is any loyalty to a mere sector of space-time. But for people like Orwell, Dickens, and Kundera, the only substitute for patriotism is attachment to some other spatiotemporal sector, to the history of something which is not a country—e.g., the history of the European novel, "the depreciated legacy of Cervantes."

20. Orwell, in *Collected Essays,* vol. 1, p. 460, says that "Even the millionaire suffers from a vague sense of guilt, like a dog eating a stolen leg of mutton. Nearly everyone, regardless of what his conduct may be, responds emotionally to the idea of human brotherhood. Dickens voiced a code which was and on the whole still is believed in, even by people who violate it. It is difficult otherwise to explain why he could be both read by working people (a thing that has happened to no other novelist of his stature) and buried in Westminister Abbey." If one had asked Dickens whether he had thought that ideal and that code inherent in human nature, or rather an historically contingent development, he would presumably have replied that he neither knew nor cared. That is the kind of question which "the wisdom of the novel" rejects as without interest or point.

21. These two quotes are from Orwell, *Collected Essays,* vol. 1, pp. 450 and 454, respectively.

22. I have argued elsewhere ("Freud and Moral Deliberation," in *The Pragmatist's Freud,* ed. Smith and Kerrigan [Baltimore: Johns Hopkins University Press, 1986]) that the increased popularity of Freudian explanations of untoward actions is an example of this changed attitude toward apparent inconsistency.

23. Byron is a good example of someone who saw the rising stock of tolerance and comfortableness as endangering the possibility of greatness. As my colleague Jerome McGann has pointed out to me, he took out this exasperation on, among other people, Cervantes: "Cervantes smiled Spain's chivalry away; / A single laugh demolished the right arm /

Of his own country;—seldom since that day / Has Spain had heroes"
(Don Juan, XIII, 11). I have not said much about the poetry-novel contrast
(as opposed to the philosophy-novel contrast) in this essay, but I would
suggest that there is as much difference between Byron and Dickens as
between either and Heidegger. That is why literature-vs.-philosophy is
too coarse-grained a contrast to be useful. Mill and Dickens, or Farrell
and Dewey, are closer to each other than Dickens is to Proust, or Byron
to Hölderlin.

Printed in the United States
38784LVS00006B/26